Gender and Employment in Rural China

T0304174

With China's rapid advancements in urbanization and industrialization, there has been significant labor movement away from agriculture in the rural regions. Using four village case studies, Song examines how this restructuring process affects the rural population.

Much of her research is centered on their various perceptions and reactions towards the market reforms. How are their lives reshaped through the employment transition? Along with the changes of family life and the diversification of development models, how do an individual's gender and background play a role in determining employment? These are the broad questions that Song addresses through detailed analysis of four different villages, in light of China's move towards decentralization of its rural economy.

Jing Song is Assistant Professor at Gender Studies Programme, The Chinese University of Hong Kong.

Routledge Contemporary China

For a full list of titles in this series, please visit www.routledge.com

Gender and Employment in Rural China

Jing Song

Routledge
Taylor & Francis Group

LONDON AND NEW YORK

First published 2017 by Routledge

2 Park Square, Milton Park, Abingdon, Oxfordshire OX14 4RN
52 Vanderbilt Avenue, New York, NY 10017

Routledge is an imprint of the Taylor & Francis Group, an informa business

First issued in paperback 2018

British Library Cataloguing-in-Publication Data
A catalogue record for this book is available from the British Library

Library of Congress Cataloging-in-Publication Data
Names: Song, Jing, 1977– author.
Title: Gender and employment in rural China / Jing Song.
Description: First Edition. | New York : Routledge, 2017. | Series:
   Routledge contemporary China series | Includes bibliographical
   references and index.
Identifiers: LCCN 2016050965 | ISBN 9781138915763 (hardback) |
   ISBN 9781315690056 (ebook)
Subjects: LCSH: Women—Employment—China. | Sex role—China. |
   Families—China. | Rural development—China—Case studies.
Classification: LCC HD6200 .S66 2017 | DDC
   331.40951/091734—dc23
LC record available at https://lccn.loc.gov/2016050965

ISBN: 978-1-138-91576-3 (hbk)
ISBN: 978-0-367-14187-5 (pbk)

Typeset in Gaillard
by Apex CoVantage, LLC

Contents

Figure

Tables

Preface

If China's urban population has recently reached 50 percent of the total, that means the other 50 percent (about 700 million people) still live in the countryside. Further, the countryside itself is urbanizing in several respects. Most important the rural economy is shifting decisively from agricultural production to other activities, creating new opportunities for residents to rethink their plans. At the same time, there is an "urbanization" of the settlement pattern in rural areas, with small villages growing into larger ones, villages into towns, towns into county seats. While leaving for the city – often one of the far away coastal cities, remains a likely option – staying in place or migrating short distances to work in a town or small city that is closer at hand is also a possibility. This means that the broad transformations of Chinese society associated with urbanization and economic development are being felt directly in the rural setting.

Jing Song offers us an inside look at how these changes are playing out in four villages. Though not a random sample, they reflect some of the important variations in rural China. Two are in coastal provinces very near to Shanghai, and they feel the influence of explosive growth in the greater Shanghai metropolitan region. The other two are described as inland, one in the interior of Hebei Province (just beyond the orbit of Beijing and Tianjin) and the other in Ningxia Province (in the suburban periphery of Yinchuan).

There is much to learn from these villages. A general question is what kinds of opportunities were created in them for peasants to transition to different kinds of work. In one case there was little potential for new local enterprises, and the main alternative to farming has continued to be labor migration. In two cases there was a general expansion of nonfarm employment but organized differently – through a mix of collective industries and private ventures that gradually became more capital-intensive in one and through local enterprises originating in village collectives in another. In yet another case, the opportunities were found less in industrial jobs and more in real estate development, via monetary compensation for expropriated land and relocation housing that could generate rental income.

A central focus of this study is how men and women responded differently and jointly to these varying situations. In the socialist period women in these villages combined a homemaker role with an active participation in agricultural collectives and later in family farms. Did rising nonfarm employment change their status? Jing Song points out that men are still considerably more likely to work in nonfarm jobs, although this option has become more available to both genders. Men are also more likely to hold jobs that offer more mobility and risk and potentially higher compensation. Hence old gender inequalities have been reproduced in the period of market reform. She takes a step beyond this male vs. female dichotomy, though, with her observation that men and women coordinate their choices in what can be understood as a family economic strategy. In a changing environment there are advantages for family members to diversify into different sectors, for one person to hold multiple jobs, or for family members to cooperate in a family-based private venture. In this study we see how these choices are made through negotiation within the family, how they evolve over time, and how revised gender norms come into being.

The main message here is that rural China is not following a single urbanizing and industrializing trajectory. There are many pathways to be taken into account at the village scale, and within villages people are continuously making and revising their choices. In this sense men and women, families, and village communities are constructing their own futures within the range of possibilities that the local context allows. As shown in many other ethnographic studies, this research depicts rural villagers who are not so much pushed into a new way of life as they are actively interpreting the situation, weighing their options, and creatively and flexibly experimenting with those choices.

John R. Logan, Brown University
September 2016

Acknowledgments

This study is developed from my doctoral dissertation at Brown University with a title of "Market Transition in China: Rural Households and Nonagricultural Employment." I want to give sincere gratitude to my supervisor, Professor John Logan, who provided numerous insightful suggestions during different stages of the writing of the dissertation. I owe thanks to other members of the dissertation committee, Professor Nancy Luke and Professor Rhacel Parrenas, for their timely advice and warm support. I also want to thank the other two readers of the dissertation, Professor Susan Short and Professor David Lindstrom, for their critical questions and probing thoughts. Professor Tamara Jacka and my anonymous reviewers also gave me important feedback in the rewriting and revision process, for which I am very grateful.

I want to thank my editor Simon Bates for his patience and kindest help during the writing and processing of the book manuscript. Shengbin Tan provided invaluable help with the preparation of the manuscript. Lulu Li spent numerous hours as my research assistant with editing and proof reading. I also wish to thank members of the research team I have been working with during the more than one decade of fieldwork in several villages in China. The research team has involved Professor Yang Shanhua, Professor Cheng Weimin, Professor Liu Xiao-jing, Professor Rodney Wai-chi Chu, Professor Patrick Pui-Lam Law, Professor Lu Huilin and other collaborating scholars. I had the honor to work with numerous colleagues in the field and benefited from our conversations: Chen Chao, Chen Wenling, Chen Yiping, Chen Zhixi, Du Jie, Feng Lu, Fu Chunhui,Gao Hongyuan, Gong Bojun,Guo Qi, Hu Feifei, Huang Huazhen, Jiang Qin, Jing Zi, Li Jiayu, Li Jing, Li Si, Li Xie, Lian Jiajia, Liang Chen, Liang Yumei, Liu Chang, Liu Limin, Liu Li, Liu Nannan, Liu Zhenzhen, Long Tengfei, Lv Fuhua, Lu Yuxia, Ma Lijuan, Peng Guangzhou, Peng Xuan, Qi Xin, Ren Qiang, Song Qian, Song Yuefei, Sun Feiyu, Tian Geng, Tian Jingwei, Tong Bin, Wang Dajun, Wang Dongjie, Wang Ke, Wang Liping, Wang Lulu, Wang Nan, Wang Xiafei, Wu Qingcao, Wu Qingyang, Xu Yuan, Yang Ke, Yang Min, Yao Jianwen, Yao Zelin, You Puyun, Yu Danxi, Yu Dong, Yu Hongqiang, Yu Hongyan, Yu Xiaoping, Zhang Dandan, Zhang Jing, Zhang Hao, Zhang Wenxia, Zhang Xun, Zhang Yan, Zhao Chao, Zhao Xiaoxue, Zheng Xiaojuan, Zhu Qian. I joined the research team when I worked with Professor Yang during my study at Peking University, and our collaboration has continued to this day with our common interests in the field of rural changes and family life.

This book incorporates contents from several papers. They include: Song, Jing and John Logan, "Family and market: nonagricultural employment in rural China," *Chinese Journal of Sociology* (CJS: Chinese), 2010, Vol. 30, No. 5, pp. 142–163; Song, Jing, "Women and self-employment in postsocialist rural China: side job, individual career or family venture," *The China Quarterly*, 2015, Vol. 221, pp. 229–242, Copyright © The China Quarterly 2015, Reprinted with permission Cambridge University Press; Song, Jing, "Official relocation and self-help development: Three housing strategies under ambiguous property rights in China's rural land development," *Urban Studies*, 2015, Vol. 52, No. 1, pp. 121–137, Copyright © 2015 by Urban Studies Journal Limited, Reprinted by permission SAGE Publications, Ltd.

My dissertation work was funded by the National Science Foundation (Doctoral Dissertation Research Improvement Grant), Beatrice and Joseph Feinberg Memorial Fund, and support from Department of Sociology, Population Studies and Teaching Center, Watson Institute for International and Public Affairs at Brown University. The follow-up fieldwork and data analyses were supported by the Research Grants Council of Hong Kong Special Administrative Region (General Research Fund, HKBU12406714), the Research Committee of Hong Kong Baptist University, and the Research Committee of the Chinese University of Hong Kong.

I want to thank Yuan Xu and my parents and in-laws for being so supportive. Anlan and Antao have taught me to think about the meaning of gender and family from a fresh perspective.

Finally, I owe my gratitude to the numerous men and women in the rural villages who shared their stories with me and other members of the research team. Their real-life experiences are the reason of the presence of this book.

1   Introduction

China has the world's largest agricultural economy, and this economy has undergone great changes, transitioning from the collective farming system to a more privatized, decentralized, and diverse economic system since the market reforms were initiated. This book aims to study the great rural transformation, in particular the employment transition from farm to nonfarm sectors under China's market-oriented reforms since the 1980s. Given rural industrialization, the increase of migration, and the rise of the private sector,[1] the fraction of the rural labor force in off-farm work grew from 15 percent in 1981 to 43 percent in 2000, within which the wage sector rose from 11 percent to 27 percent and the self-employment sector increased from 4 percent to 16 percent (Zhang, Zhang, Rozelle, & Boucher, 2006, p. 448). This book tries to provide a more recent and localized picture from a gender perspective about how the emerging opportunities of employment and social mobility were distributed among men and women in their moves into new economic sectors. Under the market reform, conflicting evidence has been documented about women's improved or disadvantaged economic positions (Bian & Logan, 1996; Liu, 2007; Michelson & Parish, 2000). Among peasants who became migrant workers and local workers in China, women counted for 31 percent of migrant workers and 36 percent of local workers in 2015 (National Bureau of Statistics of China, 2016). This book provides observations at the rural grassroots level about gender and employment transition.

The labor movement from farm to nonfarm sectors might be seen as a common phenomenon in the modernization process worldwide, with the rural population being absorbed into more "modern" economic sectors. However, China has provided a unique context for such a transition, built on a Maoist legacy of dividing the national development project into the agricultural countryside and the industrial cities, and its recent open-up policies that removed some of the institutional barriers. Although the mix of socialist redistributive powers and market forces is still under debate in China's recent modernization campaign, there is no doubt that China's reforms have led to a decline in the urban-rural divide and the monopoly of state-owned or collective-run economic unities. The market reform, however, was not a uniform process of decentralization. Official models of progress were often challenged by regional and local practices and resulted in great variations at the grassroots level, contingent on local economic and political dynamics (Friedman, 2006). This book decomposes the seemingly chaotic labor movements in different directions, to understand what is going on in contemporary rural China and how it has reshaped the lives of peasants.

The book thus focuses on not only the distinction between agricultural production and nonagricultural sectors but also the distinction within the new economic opportunities. This book does not conceptualize nonagricultural employment as necessarily an achievement, but uses the concept in a way in a typical rural environment, where nonagricultural jobs often pay more and are more highly regarded (Chen, 2005). Working in nonagricultural sectors is preferable in most cases for two reasons, related to economic welfare and social status, respectively: nonagricultural work often brings about more cash income, and nonagricultural work is likely to be conceptualized as a higher rank of job that is more decent than agricultural work. Both reasons are related to the deeply rooted divide between urban industries and rural agricultural sectors and a policy bias in favor of urban workers and residents under the socialist welfare system. However, market reforms have modified the socialist stratification system and introduced more complicated job hierarchies that need to be contextualized in different local development contexts. There are ways in which working in agriculture itself is preferable, such as stimulation by rising prices of agricultural products and the possibility of rent seeking in the land development projects. Meanwhile, not all kinds of nonagricultural work are equally desirable, and this book will differentiate different kinds of employment opportunities faced by peasants, ranging from low-paid, temporary, informal jobs to more rewarding, challenging, and prestigious work.

This book focuses on different developmental contexts, in which employment transition is a continuous process of negotiation rather than a fixed choice, evolving together with the restructuring of rural economy. This book highlights two dimensions of developmental contexts, regarding industrialization and urbanization, respectively, and the four villages under study are more or less developed regarding these two dimensions. Along with the rise of peasant incomes and "the release of hitherto underutilized labor" that dogmatically had been tied to agriculture (Unger, 1985, p. 599), different developmental pathways in villages may have brought opportunities to men and women in different ways. The investigation of employment patterns in the four villages helps to illustrate how Chinese peasants transitioned into nonfarm economic sectors, what the opportunities and obstacles are in such a transition for men and women, and how Chinese peasants interpret and evaluate this transition.

Rural development and employment transition

The socialist regime has oscillated between different agricultural policies, from the redistribution of family farms in the land reform around 1950 to the collectivization of farms in the mid- and late 1950s. The follow-up adjustments occurred in granting peasants more autonomy or tightening central control throughout the Maoist era, but within a rural-urban divide framework marked by the household registration (*hukou*) system that designated the places of residency and work. Since the early 1980s, the market reform undermined such institutional barriers that served central planning, and granted greater autonomy to peasants through the reinstatement of the family farming system. Peasants divided up the fields according to their family sizes and began to farm separately, and by the mid-1980s most rural families were "operating in a political economy of family tenancy" (Davis & Harrell, 1993, p. 2). The return from collective agriculture to the household-based production mode reshaped the incentive structures based on the dismantling of the collective property holdings and the fragmentation of land into family-managed plots (Unger, 1985, p. 595). When the state oscillated from heavy-handed control to encouragement of the autonomy of small peasant communities and households, the countryside soon celebrated the dramatically increasing agricultural productivity and household income (Nee, 1984).

Theoretically, individual peasant households have only the use rights of the farms, which are collectively owned by the rural communities. However, the family farming system has enabled peasants to strategize the use of family labor for various purposes. Given the decentralization of resource flows, rural economic activities have been diversified out of grain and into husbandry, sericulture, and orchards, and out of farming and into industrial and service sectors. These recent trends are part of the historical picture that the proportion of employees in the primary industry has been continuously shrinking since the 1950s as the result of an incremental "modernization" project, but the recent acceleration reflected the new opening processes under the market reform, although still gradual and controlled. The employment transition was accelerated at the middle of the 1980s and then at the beginning of the 1990s after Deng Xiaoping made various speeches during his famous southern tour in 1992, which resulted in policy repertoires reasserting the openness reform agenda and unleashed a wave of private entrepreneurship (Song & Logan, 2010).

Together with the redistribution of land and the acceleration of labor movement between economic sectors, another important change occurred in the governments' extraction policies. One of the goals of Chinese agricultural policies and institutions, as in many other late-developing countries, was to fund industrialization by draining agriculture and increase industrial investment based on cheap agricultural products and particularly depressed grain prices. Such state policies were backed up by strong administrative structures in a "developmental state" tradition that claimed to serve national developmental ambitions instead of local or class interests, but it contributed to the deteriorating economic situations of peasants. Suffering from the long-standing exclusion of peasants from state welfare benefits and the recent waves of land expropriation, rural areas have not only lagged behind in the development of infrastructures and welfare, but witnessed the growing rural-urban inequalities and a rural crisis at the end of the twentieth century (Chen & Chun, 2004). Over time, rural families have been left to cope with various difficulties on their own (Yan, 2011, p. 211), and employers have failed to provide benefits or care services to rural workers akin to those employers of urban workers.

In response to the loss of able laborers in agriculture and the deterioration of the rural economy, the state adopted a new "harmonious" approach to rural development in addition to the liberalization measures (Jacka & Sargeson, 2011). Governments initiated a series of agriculture-friendly policies from the end of the 1990s to the 2000s, by stabilizing the land tenures of rural households, reducing the responsibility of quota deliveries, introducing subsidies for agricultural production, and removing the agricultural tax. In addition to the emphasis on market efficiency, governments focused more on supporting the lagging-behind regions and the in-crisis farming sector. Under the official "people-centered" narrative, peasants were a vulnerable group to be taken care of rather than cheap laborers to be replaced or obstacles to be displaced to make room for development. Such measures meant to deal with the urgent problems of rural poverty and crisis and the new inequalities peasants faced despite the neoliberal celebration of the greater freedom in the market economy.

In addition to the "harmonious" approach in extraction and expropriation policies, the state proposed strategies of the integration of urban and rural areas and the construction of a "New Socialist Countryside" (*shehui zhuyi xinnongcun*) in the mid-2000s (Jacka & Sargeson, 2011; Wu, 2008). Around the same time, governments began to support the development of villages' infrastructure and the expansion of the new rural cooperative medical insurance (*xinnongcun hezuo yiliao*) and social welfare systems, including a new rural social pension insurance system (*xinxing nongcun yanglao baoxian*) and the minimum life guarantee system of rural residents (*nongcun zuidi shenghuo baozhang*), as people with a rural *hukou* had been denied access to urban welfare systems. Some other studies already found that such a "hukou" effect has declined in the reform era in the wake of enormous social and economic changes (Chan & Zhang, 1999), but it wasn't until the late 2000s that the state officially proposed to reform the hukou system under the "integrated" approach. In the move of the rural labor force to different economic sectors, it became crucial to have safety nets for the employment transition in order to ensure national stability.

Along with the restructuring of the state and collective economic sectors and the rise of the private sectors, rural economy has moved away from the long-standing separation of the agriculture-centered rural and the manufacturing-centered urban economies (Betcherman, 2004; Fleisher & Yang, 2003). However, institutional barriers and market inequalities of social and economic mobility sometimes remained and were exacerbated under the decentralization of the rural economy, which have been the target of the new government approaches of "harmonious" and "integrated" rural development. Based on the examination of the changing economic structures and job hierarchies, this book investigates how peasants take advantage of the opportunities and overcome (or fail to overcome) the difficulties. Such responses may vary between men and women, which are embedded in the gender and family norms at a grassroots level.

Gender, family, and development

How men and women respond to opportunity structures speaks to the debates on whether the market reform promotes individual choice or reinforces gender inequalities (Bian & Logan, 1996; Croll, 1983; Michelson & Parish, 2000). Historically, Chinese women and men had been segregated into different spheres: "outside" for men and "inside" for women (*Nanzhuwai, Nvzhunei*), similar to the Western breadwinner–homemaker model. Rural women's engagement in "outside" work, in particular farming, was ideally prohibited (Chen, 2004). But different from the breadwinner–homemaker model in Western countries, rural Chinese women's work involvement was still considered essential to the family, though secondary to men's. As Kabeer (1997) points out, entry into public forms of employment can bear gender-specific meanings in societies where it is socially acceptable or not for women to work outside the households. In China, traditional expectations were modified by practical concerns in different situations, and the presentation of economic activities was revised to satisfy gender-role expectations. For example, the traditional division of family labor in rural China was epitomized in the phrase "men plowing, women weaving (*nangeng nvzhi*)" (Chen, 2004), in which weaving was phrased as a family sideline activity within the confines of the households.

The socialist revolutions aimed to mobilize women into the work force (Croll, 1981, 1983; Stacey, 1983). The enhancement of women's labor participation was believed to be part of the revolutionary reconstruction of society, and gender equality in the educational system and in the labor market is closely related with the elimination of class inequalities (Blau, Ferber, & Winkler, 1986, p. 334). As a result, men and women started to work in state or collectively run organizations, and not working outside the home became the oddity (Whyte & Parish, 1984). Within two decades following the establishment of the new socialist regime, China achieved nearly universal female labor force participation (Hu, 2008). In 1987, among women aged 20 to 44 in urban China, the labor force participation rate was 90 percent (Bauer, Feng, Riley, & Zhao, 1992), whereas in Taiwan, 45.3 percent of married women aged 20 to 50 were in the labor force in 1992 (Vere & Wong, 2002). Such a contrast remains when comparing China with other East Asian societies such as Japan and South Korea. In the Maoist era, women's labor force participation was highly valued, not only to liberate women from the patriarchal feudal system, but also to mobilize labor during the labor shortage periods (Andors, 1983; Hu, 2008).

Despite the Maoist ideology of gender equality, gendered work was a constant principle of organization in the countryside (Hershatter, 2011) that assumed men's heavy work and women's light work (Bossen, 2002, p. 98). In rural areas, women working in agricultural collectives systematically earned fewer work points (*gongfen*) than men (Wolf, 1985). From this perspective, the socialist revolution on gender relations was more successful in urban areas, where both spouses were expected to work full-time as assigned by work units and earn comparable wages based on the Chinese government's "equal pay" policy (Hu, 2008,

p. 4). As such, China's socialism transformed the previous private form of patri-archy to a public form of "state patriarchy" in which women were still subordi-nated to the interests of the nation and the family (Stacey, 1983). Furthermore, women's household responsibilities were not called into question by the social-ist regime (Honig & Hershatter, 1988; Jacka, 1990). Women were still more likely to be the homemaker (Chen, 2004) and they had to shoulder the so-called "double burden": full-time work and home responsibilities. As a result, women tended to make their work schedules more flexible and compatible with family responsibilities.

In the reform era, the socialist gender equalization programs of labor partici-pation have been further undermined in both urban and rural areas. In urban areas, more women retreated from formal jobs and chose to be housewives (Hu, 2008). In rural areas, the dismantling of collective farms had pushed women into family farms, reflecting a return of women from the public forms of employment to the economic activities that are inside, flexible, and more compatible with family responsibilities. In general, men disproportionately moved out of family farming and entered the wage sector or ran private business (Chen, 2004), while women tended to take over the less valued farm work (Croll, 1983; de Brauw, Li, Liu, Rozelle, & Zhang, 2008; Entwisle & Henderson, 2000; Jacka, 1997; Judd, 1990), which was "feminized" and redefined as "inside work" (Chen, 2004). According to the China National Rural Survey, the total off-farm employment ratio had increased from 16 percent in 1981 to 48 percent in 2000 for rural peo-ple in China, which increased from 27 percent to 63 percent for men and 4 per-cent to 31 percent for women (Zhang, de Brauw, & Rozelle, 2004). Both men and women have become involved in off-farm employment in greater propor-tions over time, which lends support to de Brauw's finding about the declining proportion of farm work for both men and women (de Brauw, 2003). Never-theless, rural men continued to be disproportionately represented in the wage sector, whereas women were overrepresented in agricultural fieldwork (Chen, 2004). At the national level it remains unclear whether the gender gap is closing or enhancing in employment transition into different economic sectors and jobs.

The different types of work have created new room for men and women as well as features of gender-specific obstacles (Jacka, 1997, 2005; Judd, 1994, 2002). For rural women who had been excluded from urban wage jobs, many found new opportunities in rural-to-urban migration (Jacka & Song, 2004) and rural enterprises (township and village enterprises, or TVEs) (Croll, 1983; Jacka, 1997). Nevertheless, women also tended to concentrate in low-paid manufacturing jobs and were confronted with market discrimination, harsh working conditions, and sexual exploitation. Along with the restructuring of the rural and urban economy, achievement and competition in the private sector have been increasingly related with masculinity, while stable wage work is feminized for its passivity (Rofel, 1999). Jacka (1997) charts the changes in the gender division of labor in rural China and traces the social construction of women's work under dichotomies of "outside" and "inside," "heavy" and "light," and sometimes "skilled" and "unskilled," with the first element in each pair associated with men and the second with women.

Such perceptions were related to the revival of patriarchal traditions as well as the withdrawal of the state control on gender equalization programs (Croll, 1983). In short, both the Maoist and the reform eras failed to eliminate gender inequalities but reshaped gendered meanings of work in different forms.

The gendered meanings of work are to be contextualized in families in which men and women coordinate their different goals and common interests in finding a job. The family coordination of economic activities has remained important in China's countryside, and housework and care work have been rarely outsourced in rural areas. As the employment transitions take place together with the economic restructuring of rural China, family strategies provide a unique angle of how people read opportunities and how the family coordinates economic activities differently. As the norm of working in collective agriculture is replaced by a household-based calculation of labor investment, men and women need to negotiate work patterns as partners, and the dismantling of collective farms may have given rise to the previously oppressed patriarchal traditions that favor men's outside work. Furthermore, cooperation and tensions also occur across generations.

Despite the neoliberal celebration of market expansion and economic opening up, changes in employment patterns are neither linear nor uniform. It has been common for people to move back and forth between different categories of work, such as farming, local wage jobs, migrant work, or private business. Meanwhile, peasant households tended to hold multiple jobs in different economic spheres. Although most rural households had some member working off the farm, the majority of them kept one foot in the farming sector (Jacka, 2012; Van der Ploeg & Ye, 2010). Depending on their understandings of the prestigious, lucrative, or "appropriate" jobs, the family may adopt a diversification strategy in which different family members are involved in different types of employment; a multitasking strategy in which the same family member is engaged in several types of employment simultaneously; or a family-cooperation strategy in which family members cooperate in the same venture. Such responses were shaped by the evolving economic structures, which vary across regions in terms of the attractiveness of the farming sector, the availability of local wage jobs, the resources to run private businesses, or the exposure to labor markets at a distance. As such, this book takes into consideration distinct developmental contexts to examine how individuals and families respond to opportunity structures.

Diversity in Chinese villages

The book describes four village case studies based on two key modernization processes, industrialization and urbanization, because these two processes have shaped the employment transition patterns in important ways that are gendered and village specific. Based on the diverse contexts in which the employment transitions have taken place, rural communities experienced economic expansion in distinct ways that redefined the relationships between agriculture and nonagricultural economic sectors, that of local and migrant employment opportunities, and that between collective assets and private resources. This book does not aim to find extreme cases of villages at the ends of development continua on their overall economic performances, as most rural communities are still in a process of change. Instead, this book treats China's vast countryside as characterized by different combinations of socialist legacies, patriarchal traditions, and market forces, and the village cases were selected to speak for such important variations in local developmental pathways (how the industrialization and urbanization processes have been carried out differently), as well as the gendered experiences in economic expansion. This book uses four villages as field sites, featured by different processes of industrialization and urbanization, as the setting in which employment patterns have been shaped. The four villages are selected from the provinces of Hebei (Han Village), Ningxia (Ning Village), Jiangsu (Su Village), and Zhejiang (Bei Village). Pseudonyms are used for people and locations at or below the county and district levels.

The selection of the villages serves to present the difference in developmental pathways between the interior part of China (two villages) and the coastal areas (two villages). The interior and coastal divergence was first embedded in the inland dryland farming system and the coastal grain-growing sectors, respectively. The coastal areas witnessed higher population density and land scarcity, and these areas have historically been engaged in sideline activities such as the production of silk, wine, tea, and other textile products based on their close connection with urban manufacturing bases and consumption hubs. Both coastal and inland villages had been dominated by collective farming throughout the Maoist era, while in the reform era, peasants faced different developmental pathways that allowed them to leave farms.

Industrialization is the first dimension that differentiates local development patterns. In the early reform years, the governments first opened up coastal cities and special economic zones in the coastal areas, and the coastal countryside witnessed an early exposure to market forces. In areas such as the Yangtze River Delta, the grassroots entrepreneurial dynamics had contributed to an early start of rural industrialization. For the areas characterized by early rural industrialization, some witnessed the development of the township and village enterprises (TVEs) with strong local state direction and collective intervention (mainly represented by the "Sunan" model in the south of Jiangsu Province). Some other areas were characterized by the prosperity of family-owned businesses (particularly as in the "Wenzhou" model, which emerged in a coastal city of Zhejiang).[2] The selection of the two coastal villages is based on the different industrialization pathways, regarding the roles of collective and private economic sectors, including family business and self-employment. Such rising economic sectors absorbed rural men and women in great scales, and these women have deviated from the conventional image of women who migrate and join the docile labor pool of "working sisters" (*dagongmei*) or the left-behind women who take care of farms.

The boundary between different models of rural industrialization built on collective coordination or private accumulation has been blurred because of the privatization of TVEs and the infusion of global capital, but such legacies still had an impact on employment patterns. In Bei Village (Zhejiang Province), the rural industrialization process was driven by both collective enterprises and private businesses, in which sideline activities and family accumulations had played an important role. In Su Village (Jiangsu Province), the village economy is dominated by a few big enterprises, which used to be collectively run and remained in close connection with the village collective leadership after privatization. These early industrialized rural areas also witnessed urban sprawl into the countryside as part of the modernization process, but the rural-urban income gap has been narrowed due to the rural industrialization and commercialization processes. The urbanization and land development projects only played a secondary role in pulling peasants away from agricultural sectors, because industrialization had already done so in the early reform years.

The second dimension, urbanization, has been more important in inland areas that lacked the local industrial and entrepreneurial dynamics. In these areas, out-migration to distant urban jobs has been the dominant ways of employment transition, and peasants are divided into migrants and the "left-behind" who keep their land cultivated. Agriculture remains important for sustaining peasants' livelihood, and migrants maintain a tie with their land based on regular returns from migrant work. Furthermore, the central state has adopted subsidies and policies to support agricultural production nationwide, and more favors were given to inland and frontier regions to protect not only farmland but also grassland and forests, for the sake of multiple goals, including grain sufficiency, social stability, and environmental sustainability. But under the recent national strategy to develop western China, land development has become an important economic engine for local governments to "catch up with" the coastal regions. This leads to the divergence between inland villages from which villagers continue to migrate to cities for job opportunities and those in which the expanding city comes to the villagers.

The book uses two inland villages, Han Village and Ning Village, where rural entrepreneurial dynamics are much more limited than in their coastal counterparts. Han's economy (Hebei Province) heavily relies on labor migration to urban centers, which has resulted in the commonly observed division of family labor between the outflow of "quality labor" and the staying of less able people, although migrants retain a close connection to the community and return home frequently. In contrast, Ning Village (Ningxia Province) experienced massive land development in recent decades. Because land had been an important fallback position for migrant workers, villagers have been anxious about how to relocate their means of living in the face of land expropriation. In addition to the reshuffling of economic structures and job opportunities following land development, many villagers in Ning Village had turned to their new property-holding positions as a source of generating income, and the division of labor within families also evolved accordingly.

Figure 1.1 illustrates the distinct positions of the four villages in the industrialization and urbanization processes. The selection of villages first of all reflects the difference between those with and without an early and locally based industrialization process (between coastal and inland areas), and then how the

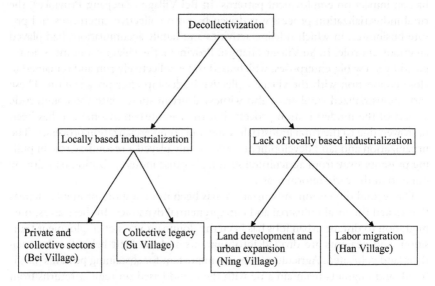

Figure 1.1 Four villages in the industrialization and urbanization processes

industrialization process has been carried out (between two coastal villages) and whether urbanization projects have been introduced in "lagging behind" areas (between two inland villages). As for the two coastal villages, the industrialization process is heavily influenced by collective legacy in Su Village but is increasingly dominated by the rise of the private sector in Bei Village. As for the two inland villages, the land development projects in Ning Village have greatly accelerated the urbanization process and the transplantation of external employers, whereas most people in Han Village still rely on migration to access nonagricultural jobs. Both the early rural industrialization waves and the more recent urbanization processes aimed to modernize the countryside, and the different directions and paces of these modernization campaigns have shaped distinct relationships between farm and nonfarm work, locally based and migration-based economies, or family cooperation and extra-household economic sectors in these areas.

First, the relationship between farm and nonfarm work differs not only between the coastal and inland villages but also within these two areas. Although the economic significance of farming has in general decreased, peasants still have various reasons to cherish land and maintain their bond to farms, due either to memories from historical periods of turmoil and famine or to concerns of economic security to deal with market uncertainties of nonfarm work with farming as a fallback position. In cases of land scarcity, the low land-population ratio may either push the labor force out of the farming sector or result in a highly labor-intensive farming system and strong attachment to land. Similarly, the low agricultural productivity may contribute to a careless attitude toward land, but peasants may continue to multitask across agricultural and nonagricultural sectors. Furthermore, there are other economic incentives that could reinforce peasants' motivation to invest in farms or maintain the land entitlement, including the implementation of pro-agriculture policies and subsidies, the establishment of commercial agriculture projects, or the rise of land prices. Meanwhile, farming tasks have become lighter due to the technological advancement, which facilitated the diversification of the peasant–farm bond given the different exposure to labor markets.

With regard to rural industrialization, compared with the early industrialized coastal villages, inland villages may see farming as more important due to the limited economic opportunities. Agriculture in the inland areas had been less labor-intensive with limited outputs, but people may keep one foot in the farming sector so as to receive agricultural subsidies. However, the lack of "local" jobs may have forced inland peasants to move for external migrant jobs, and their commitment to farming was inevitably season-based, whereas coastal peasants may be able to multitask and switch between farm and off-farm work more easily given the presence of local job opportunities. With regard to urbanization, land development brings about changes in land assignment, property rights, and employment structures, which may detach peasants from land. But with the increase of land price, peasants may have stronger incentives to maintain control of land and to increase their investment in farming in exchange for more compensation. The rediscovering of land values may have led to variations in the "lagging areas" in terms of whether they should leave land behind or maintain and invest in land more intensively.

Second, the different developmental pathways have created diverse relationships between local jobs and migrant work. The massive rural-to-urban migration flows have been extensively studied with a focus on their impact on urban economies and the experiences of migrants (Fan, 2008; Jacka, 2006; Solinger, 1999), or how migration has changed rural communities of origin (Jacka, 2012; Murphy, 2002). Such migration has been gendered and dominated by men and young women who are perceived to be more mobile, whereas women often felt torn between the two worlds of external labor markets and family obligations back home (Jacka, 2006). For both men and women, it is difficult to settle down in cities, and more often they become a group of "strangers" in the city (Zhang, 2001) who would eventually return to where they came from.

Compared with migrant work, less attention has been paid to local opportunities emerging in rural communities, which could be in the form of local state-directed industrialization or the rise of private businesses, or in a form driven by government-initiated urbanization or self-development of land and housing (Song, 2015). For example, rural industrialization created local job opportunities that were different from urban work units, and they tended to be less institutionalized and more flexible in job arrangements. Although rural nonagricultural sectors have been positioned low in the previous job hierarchies compared with the urban state and collective sectors, both the urban-rural boundary and the public-private sector divides have been modified. Furthermore, urbanization may create more local job opportunities and transplant new employers into the locality. In such processes, personal choices and family strategies have evolved together with the restructuring of the rural economy in which many peasants gained more confidence in their own entrepreneurial activities both within and beyond rural communities.

Third, the roles of family cooperation and extra-household operations of economic activities vary due to the different industrialization and urbanization patterns. The concept of the "household" is crucial to the understanding of smallholder peasant economies, and in China it has remained important, especially under the reinstated household-based farming system. The concept of family sometimes overlaps with that of the household, but families emphasize a combination of marriage, kinship, and economic relations, whereas households refer to similar units but based more on residence, production, and commensality (Jacobs, 2010). Family members may move out of the household for migrant work or business, but they also cooperate within the household in their rural base. Different from an urban setting where people typically expect to have formal wage work based on qualifications outside the home, rural people may be engaged in less "formal" family business or self-employment characterized by more flexible job arrangements, unstable incomes, and a chance to "become one's own boss." In some areas, however, peasants rely more on external employers outside the home to get wage jobs. In coastal villages where rural industries prospered under collective coordination, the collective-based economy was more important in mobilizing resources than private accumulations. Such rural industries have evolved and generated more institutionalized career ladders comparable to urban economic sectors, and their employees have been positioned in factory regimes or workplaces different from those of family coordination. The situation is similar for rural migrant workers from inland villages, but their workplaces are characterized by different working conditions and entrepreneurial dynamics.

Both family cooperation and external employers can provide economic opportunities for rural men and women. Some people choose to work within the household confines for the greater flexibility and profitability, but households are sites both of unity and of dissension (Sen, 1990), as well as of oppression and exploitation of women (Jacobs, 2010). In gender terms, women may have been engaged in family business for greater freedom, but it may also lead women to return to the family sphere with a "market-supported naturalization of women's roles" (Evans, 2010). Women's agency within family coordinated economic activities, however, is vague due to the mixed norms and coexisting expectations for women to be good earners and good homemakers. Similar nuanced views have been adopted to study rural women's positions in wage sectors, that they are empowered by their cash-earning power (Zhang, 2007) but are subject to new forms of exploitations in factory regimes as a cheap and manageable labor force (Fan, 2003). The real-life understandings of employment opportunities and constraints for men and women are to be studied in localities with different combinations of within- and extra-household economies.

In sum, this book uses an integrated approach to incorporate developmental contexts and family strategies in the analysis of employment patterns. From the top-down perspective, macro-level policy repertoires are implemented at the discretion of local offices, with different support for rural industries and diverse resources and connections people can draw on. From the bottom-up perspective, villagers respond to the changing opportunity structures but also make initiatives based on their resources, connections, experiences, and skills, although still constrained by their values and understandings to take full advantage of the open-up policies. Such grassroots initiatives in turn affect the local opportunity structures and employment patterns, via their interactions with governments, local cadres, developers, and other market forces. By contextualizing changes in employment patterns in the four villages, this book examines how rural men and women are not only constrained by resource limits and traditional beliefs but also respond to opportunity structures in creative ways, not only as market competitors but also as family coordination partners.

Fieldwork and the four villages under study

The field visits were paid to rural households, and during the visits, either the husband or the wife was interviewed as the main respondent to talk about not only their work trajectories but also how their work was paired between spouses and coordinated within the household. If possible, both spouses were interviewed. Interviews lasted one to two hours, conducted individually, mostly in interviewees' homes. For cases in which both spouses were interviewed, many of them were interviewed separately during the researchers' multiple visits, and there were some situations where both spouses were interviewed together, but it occurred frequently that one of the spouses often joined the conversation in the middle when he or she arrived home or left the conversation in the middle to run other errands. In general, the individual narratives of respondents seemed not affected by the presence or absence of their spouses. Most interviews were audio-recorded with permission from respondents. Pseudonyms are used for the locations at or below the county level, as well as for some archives and website links that are quoted and may reveal the names of locations or people, to assure the anonymity and confidentiality of respondents.

Bei Village is located in coastal Zhejiang Province. As other south coastal villages, Bei Village has a long grain-growing history, while at the same time some peasant households specialized in wine making and fishing as an important source of family income. But such family sideline activities had been suppressed under the collective farming system throughout the Maoist era. The decollectivization of farms was implemented in the early 1980s, and collective enterprises in wine making, textile and other manufacturing sectors also mushroomed, along with the rapid growth of private businesses and household workshops in the following decades. Though the wet rice cultivation is labor intensive, many peasants have engaged in part-time or full-time work in local enterprises, and began to rent or outsource their farmland to managerial farmers or migrant workers. The local industries also absorbed migrant workers from inland rural areas, and many locals have become entrepreneurs and businesspersons whose economic activities transcended the boundary of the local market. Both men and women have been active in wage work and private businesses, and some women have chosen to be stay-at-home mothers recently. Meanwhile, the use of land has proceeded with caution, except under the city's urban planning project that rezoned most of the village land into the greenbelt of the city[3] and further undermined the importance of the farming sector.

Su Village is in coastal Jiangsu Province. With an established tradition of growing grain, peasants had been primarily engaged in agricultural work under collective organizations (communes or production teams) throughout the 1950s and the 1960s. Similar to Bei Village, the grassroots initiative of industrialization began to emerge as the state loosened control over the local economy. However, the nascent industries were less related to the traditional sidelines and craftsmanship but more modeled after urban manufactory centers. In this industrialization process, the local office and cadres played an essential role, and the "getting rich" efforts had been primarily a collective behavior, until the privatization movement in the 1990s. The big local enterprises absorbed most local laborers, and it was not common for villagers to migrate for external jobs or run private businesses. Under the legacy of collective patronage, the local office has coordinated the projects of managerial farming and organized collective housing construction projects, so that each household could get a single-family house at a low price.

Han Village is located in Hebei Province with a distance of a three-hour drive from Beijing. Compared with the grain-growing system in the two coastal villages, Han Village is typical of the dryland farming system with a lower population density. Constrained by the access to water, peasants tend to grow wheat, corn, soybean, peanut, and sometimes cotton, with fewer crop cycles and less labor investment. The use of machinery made the farming tasks lighter but did not increase the agricultural productivity and income greatly. Related to this, the local policies on land use have been loose, and the informal land transfer has been conducted at low prices. Some peasant households have rented part of their land to quarries for a period of several years, and in addition to these quarries, there have been little local industries to accommodate local laborers. Meanwhile, the proximity of urban centers facilitated villagers to become migrant workers, especially men and young women. Married women and the elderly usually stayed to take care of farms and conduct home-based sidelines, but some women also became tied movers who would migrate together with their husbands to seek jobs.

Ning Village in Ningxia Province used to be in a similar position as Han Village given the dryland farming system and a lack of local entrepreneurial dynamics. Peasants had relied on a mix of farming, migrant work, and petty family businesses such as raising livestock, food processing, and transportation to sustain their livelihood. Since the 1990s, Ning Village has been included in a series of large land development projects initiated by the municipality government and other developers. With their land taken away to construct industrial zones, commercial centers, and residential areas, peasants became "urban residents" overnight. The rapid urbanization process deprived peasants of land and transplanted enterprises and companies with more local work opportunities. But the labor movement from agricultural to nonagricultural sectors has been selective, which marginalized many villagers who were aged or with limited education. Meanwhile, they felt the pressure to find income-generating opportunities to finance their urban lives and individual urban homes for the next generations.

The four villages have been visited repeatedly from 2001 to 2011 by the research team led by Professor Yang Shanhua and other scholars at Peking University. The research team has mainly used a snowball-sampling strategy to find respondents and followed up on the solicited referrals to gain a relatively even coverage of socioeconomic status in each rural community rather than sampling from a narrow social circle. Respondents were asked about their experiences and expectations about their work trajectories and how they were coordinated within the family. Some respondents were interviewed multiple times and provided a more complete narrative of their engagement in various economic activities over time. The interviews were coded by the emerging themes of the types of work, including home-based sideline work, migrant work, local wage work, family businesses, and so on, and their stories shed light on the mechanisms by which economic opportunities were distributed in a transitional economy.

The author also used local archives and interviews with local officials to gain information on economic structures and local politics. Their variations resulted from not only locations and resources, but also the processes of policy implementation and grassroots reactions during industrialization and urbanization. Economic structures, together with developmental pathways, helped to shape what kind of skills and qualities are valued in the labor market and how work experiences may be different for men and women. By seeing employment as a choice negotiated at the household level and as an issue of job selectivity shaped by the market setting, this book relates the diversification of career paths and job mobility to family work patterns and the local sources of prosperity. Table 1.1 summarises the characteristics of the four villages at the time of investigation.

Structure of the book

Chapter 1 has introduced the massive rural transformation of employment patterns due to the transition from collective agriculture to a more privatized, decentralized, and diverse rural economy. It begins with historical backgrounds with regard to rural development in China, and then discusses its relationship with gender roles and family division of labor. Then it moves on to explain the selection of four villages under investigation and how they represented different developmental contexts with regard to industrialization and urbanization processes. The chapter lays out the framework to study the different patterns of employment transition between agricultural and nonagricultural, local and migrant, or family-based and other economic sectors.

Chapter 2 provides theoretical discussions based on existing studies on peasants, gender roles, and family division of labor in rural China. Peasants have been positioned in a dichotomy of urban cores and rural peripheries in modernization theories, and there have been debates on how to read their rational choices or survival strategies. Although being frequently described as passive and conservative,

Table 1.1 Characteristics of the four villages at the time of investigation

Village province	Households, population	Rural income per capita in the region (RMB)	Conventional cropping patterns	Post-reform industrialization	Urbanization
Bei Village, Zhejiang (coastal)	456 households, 1128 persons	12026[1]	Grain and others	Early industrialization with private and collective sectors	Gradual
Su village, Jiangsu (coastal)	427 households, 1697 persons	12969[2]	Grain and others	Early industrialization dominated by collective enterprises	Gradual
Han Village, Hebei (inland)	312 households, 1315 persons	4682[3]	Wheat, corn, and others	Late	No
Ning Village, Ningxia (inland)	524 households, 3826 persons	4917[4]	Wheat, corn, and others	Late	Rapid

Note: [1] For the year 2009, the Shaoxing Local Archive Office (Shaoxing shi difangzhi bangongshi), 2014. *Shaoxing Yearbook 2014 (Shaoxing nianjian 2014)*. Fangzhi Publisher (Fangzhi chubanshe), the color page.

[2] For the year 2009, Suzhou Bureau of Statistics (Suzhou shi tongjiju), 2010. *Comparable analysis of villagers' life in Suzhou, Changzhou, Wuxi (Suxichang sanshi nongminshengbuozhuangkuang bijiaofenxi)*. Retrieved September 27, 2016 from www.sztjj.gov.cn/info_detail.asp?id=19075

[3] For the year 2009, Baoding Bureau of Statistics (Baoding shi tongjiju), 2010. *Baoding Economic and Social Development Statistics Report 2009 (Baoding shi 2009nian guominjingji be shehuifazhan tongjigongbao)*. Retrieved August 15, 2016 from www.bdtj.gov.cn/shownews.asp?nid=49

[4] For the year 2008, Yinchuan Bureau of Statistics (Yinchuan shi tongjiju), 2010. *Yinchuan Economic and Social Development Statistics Report 2008 (Yinchuan shi 2008nian guominjingji be shehuifazhan tongjigongbao)*. Retrieved July 28, 2016 from www.tjcn.org/tjgb/201001/3334_2.html

Chinese peasants have been praised as the driving force of economic development, but also faced new inequalities and exploitations, as shown by theories in the Marxist traditions. Similarly, rural women have been portrayed as a vulnerable and "left-behind" group in market reforms. Such gender inequalities failed to be solved by the Marxist agenda of gender equalization that promoted gender sameness in paid work, or by the neoliberal campaign of self-development. As the job hierarchies have been restructuring, women's (and men's) agency should be studied by taking into consideration their flexibility in moving between a great variety of formal and informal economic activities within and beyond households. The existing theorizations of the mixed dynamics of individualization and householding suggest that employment is negotiated and contested based on different normative and practical concerns, and such family strategies need to be further contextualized in the localized developmental contexts in contemporary China.

Chapters 3–6 examine the emergence and evolvement of economic opportunities for men and women in each village and how individuals and families cooperate in economic activities. By exploring the relationship between developmental politics and family strategies, these chapters illustrate the diverse forms of gendered employment transition. The two coastal villages have witnessed different industrialization processes given the different meanings of "modern" sectors. In Bei Village, both sideline activities and collective industries have contributed to rural industrialization, and the two converged under the rise of private sectors, in which "being one's own boss" became most prestigious in the new job hierarchy, while family cooperation remained important in accommodating men's and women's aspirations. In Su Village, the industrialization process has been heavily influenced by collective legacy. Although the big collective enterprises have been privatized, they continued to accommodate the majority of local employees. The availability of local white-collar jobs empowered young and educated locals in the labor market, but the gender division of labor was reproduced in the more institutionalized career ladders in workplace and in household chores and care work across generations at home.

Compared with the two coastal villages with early locally based industrialization processes, the two inland villages lacked rural entrepreneurial dynamics. In Han Village, labor migration remained dominant in providing opportunities in nonagricultural sectors. "Male bonding" became important in mobilizing the limited resources in running family businesses but was constrained due to market segregation and the fragmentation of common interests among villagers. In Ning Village, the land development projects greatly accelerated the urbanization process, but the transplantation of external employers did not necessarily favor locals as potential employees. Although women and men began to adapt to low-end individual jobs in the city, they also turned to rent seeking as a major source of income based on their compensation and relocation gains. Such economic reconfiguration occurred in parallel with demographic and residential changes in the family sphere, which also affected the family division of labor in the four villages.

Chapter 7 summarizes that the four case studies regarding important variations in developmental contexts, including policies and practices on land use and its relationship with other economic sectors, the relationship between local structures of life chances and migration-based economy, and the structure of career ladders and the means of job mobility. The four villages illustrated different combinations of the farm and nonfarm, local and migrant, extra-household and family-based components of a transitional economy. Accordingly, employment is a continuing process rather than a fixed choice, and families are in a process of adapting their strategies with changing political and economic environments. Depending on developmental politics, women might have started their market adventure as docile laborers and sideline workers, yet new employment opportunities and challenges were created by the restructuring of economic sectors, the evolving ideologies of gender roles, and the changing systems of family and village properties.

Notes

1   The numbers of private businesses have increased from 0.14 million in 1978 to 27 million individual businesses and 5.5 million private enterprises in 2007 (Huang 2008). In rural areas, self-employment has been the fastest growing off-farm sector, making up 40 percent of all new off-farm jobs from 1988 to 1995. (Zhang et al. 2006, p. 446).
2   Zhao (2004) differentiated how different labor regimes were related to different kinds of qualities of individual laborers, in the "coastal laissez-faire provinces" (where more employees exist in household/private enterprises than in local government enterprises), the "coastal corporatist provinces" (where there are more employees in local government enterprises than in individual and private enterprises), and finally the "inland provinces" area (where people heavily rely on external employers for employment).
3   Greenbelt zones are designed in some Chinese cities as part of the project to beautify the urban landscape. The city government may assign such suburban greenbelt zones to be public entertaining areas or parks to make the city more "green."

References

Andors, P. (1983). *The unfinished liberation of Chinese women, 1949–1980*. Bloomington: Indiana University Press.
Bauer, J., Feng, W., Riley, N. E., & Zhao, X. H. (1992). Gender inequality in urban China: Education and employment. *Modern China, 18*(3), 333–370.
Betcherman, G. (2004, April 29). *Labour market reform in China: How 700 million Chinese workers are coping with global capitalism*. Sefton Memorial Lecture, University of Toronto, Toronto, Canada.
Bian, Y., & Logan, J. R. (1996). Market transition and the persistence of power: The changing stratification system in urban China. *American Sociological Review, 1996*, 739–758.
Blau, F., Ferber, M., & Winkler, A. (1986). *The economics of women, men and work*. Englewood Cliffs, NJ: Prentice-Hall.
Bossen, L. (2002). *Chinese women and rural development: Sixty years of change in Lu Village, Yunnan*. Lanham, MD: Rowman and Littlefield.

Chan, K. W., & Zhang, L. (1999). The hukou system and rural-urban migration in China: Processes and changes. *The China Quarterly, 160*, 818–855.

Chen, F. (2004). The division of labor between generations of women in rural China. *Social Science Research, 33*(4), 557–580.

Chen, F. (2005). Employment transitions and the household division of labor in China. *Social Forces, 84*(2), 831–851.

Chen, G. D., & Chun, T. (2004). *Zhongguo nongmin diaocha (An investigative report of the Chinese peasantry)*. Beijing: People's Literature Publishing House.

Croll, E. J. (1981). *The politics of marriage in contemporary China*. Cambridge: Cambridge University Press.

Croll, E. J. (1983). *Chinese women since Mao*. Armonk, NY: M.E. Sharpe.

Davis, D., & Harrell, S. (1993). *Chinese families in the post-Mao era*. Berkeley: University of California Press.

de Brauw, A. (2003). *Are women taking over the farm in China?* Paper provided by Department of Economics, Williams College, in its series Department of Economics Working Papers, 199.

de Brauw, A., Li, Q., Liu, C., Rozelle, S., & Zhang, L. (2008). Feminization of agriculture in China? Myths surrounding women's participation in farming. *The China Quarterly, 194*, 327–348.

Entwisle, B., & Henderson, G. (2000). *Re-drawing boundaries: Work, households, and gender in China* (Vol. 25). Berkeley: University of California Press.

Evans, H. (2010). The gender of communication: Changing expectations of mothers and daughters in urban China. *The China Quarterly, 204*, 980–1000.

Fan, C. C. (2003). Rural-urban migration and gender division of labor in transitional China. *International Journal of Urban and Regional Research, 27*(1), 24–47.

Fan, C. C. (2008). China on the move: Migration, the state, and the household. *The China Quarterly, 196*, 924–956.

Fleisher, B., & Yang, D. T. (2003). Labor laws and regulations in China. *China Economic Review, 14*, 426–433.

Friedman, S. (2006). *Intimate politics: Marriage, the market, and state power in southeastern China*. Cambridge, MA: Harvard University Press.

Hershatter, G. (2011). *The gender of memory: Rural women and China's collective past*. Berkeley: University of California Press.

Honig, E., & Hershatter, G. (1988). *Personal voices: Chinese women in the 1980's*. Stanford, CA: Stanford University Press.

Hu, C. Y. (2008). *A longitudinal study of married women's probability of being housewives in reforming urban China*. Unpublished doctoral dissertation, Department of Sociology, Louisiana State University, Baton Rouge, U.S.

Huang, M. (ed.) (2008). *Zhongguo minying jingji fazhan baogao (The development report of non-state-owned economy in China)*. Beijing: Social Sciences Academic Press.

Jacka, T. (1990). Back to the wok: Women and employment in Chinese industry in the 1980s. *The Australian Journal of Chinese Affairs, 24*, 1–23.

Jacka, T. (1997). *Women's work in rural China: Change and continuity in an era of reform*. Cambridge: Cambridge University Press.

Jacka, T. (2005). Finding a place: Negotiations of modernization and globalization among rural women in Beijing. *Critical Asian Studies, 37*(1), 51–74.

Jacka, T. (2006). *Rural women in urban China: Gender, migration and social change*. Armonk, NY: M.E. Sharpe.

Jacka, T. (2012). Migration, householding and the well-being of left-behind women in rural Ningxia. *China Journal, 67,* 1–22.

Jacka, T., & Sargeson, S. (Eds.). (2011). *Women, gender and rural development in China.* Northampton, MA: Edward Elgar Publishing.

Jacka, T., & Song, X. (2004). My life as a migrant worker. In A. M. Gaetano & T. Jacka (Eds.), *On the move: Women and rural-to-urban migration in contemporary China* (pp. 286–307). New York: Columbia University Press.

Jacobs, J. (2010). *Gender and agrarian reforms.* London and New York: Routledge.

Judd, E. R. (1990). Alternative development strategies for women in rural China. *Development and Change, 21*(1), 23–42.

Judd, E. R. (1994). *Gender and power in rural North China.* Stanford, CA: Stanford University Press.

Judd, E. R. (2002). *The Chinese women's movement between state and market.* Stanford, CA: Stanford University Press.

Kabeer, N. (1997). Women, wages and intra-household power relations in Urban Bangladesh. *Development and Change, 28*(2), 261–302.

Liu, J. (2007). *Gender and work in urban China: Women workers of the unlucky generation.* London and New York: Routledge.

Michelson, E., & Parish, W. (2000). Gender differentials in economic success: Rural China in 1991. In B. Entwisle & G. Henderson (Eds.), *Redrawing boundaries: Gender, households, and work in China* (pp. 134–156). Berkeley: University of California Press.

Murphy, R. (2002). *How migrant labor is changing rural China.* Cambridge: Cambridge University Press.

National Bureau of Statistics of China. (2016). *2015 survey reports of peasant workers (2015nian nongmingong jiancediaochabaogao).* Retrieved October 5, 2016, from www.stats.gov.cn/tjsj/zxfb/201604/t20160428_1349713.html

Nee, V. (1984). Peasant household individualism. *International Journal of Sociology, 14*(4), 50–76.

Rofel, L. (1999). *Other modernities: Gendered yearnings in China after socialism.* Berkeley: University of California Press.

Sen, A. (1990). Gender and cooperative conflicts. In I. Inker (Ed.), *Persistent inequalities* (pp. 123-149). Oxford: Oxford University Press.

Solinger, D. J. (1999). *Contesting citizenship in urban China: Peasant migrants, the state, and the logic of the market.* Berkeley: University of California Press.

Song, J. (2015). Official relocation and self-help development: Three housing strategies under ambiguous property rights in China's rural land development. *Urban Studies, 52*(1), 121–137.

Song, J., & Logan, J. (2010). Family and market: Nonagricultural employment in rural China. *Chinese Journal of Sociology, 30*(5), 142–163.

Stacey, J. (1983). *Patriarchy and socialist revolution in China.* Berkeley: University of California Press.

Unger, J. (1985). The decollectivization of the Chinese countryside: A survey of twenty-eight villages. *Pacific Affairs, 58*(4), 585–606.

Van der Ploeg, J. D., & Ye, J. Z. (2010). Multiple job holding in rural villages and the Chinese road to development. *The Journal of Peasant Studies, 37*(3), 513–530.

Vere, J., & Wong, G. (2002). *Women's labor force participation and occupational choice in Taiwan.* Retrieved March 4, 2017 from citeseerx.ist.psu.edu/viewdoc/download?doi=10.1.1.533.5959&rep=rep1&type=pdf

Whyte, M. K., & Parish, W. L. (1984). *Urban life in contemporary China*. Chicago: University of Chicago Press.

Wolf, M. (1985). *Revolution postponed: Women in contemporary China*. Stanford, CA: Stanford University Press.

Wu, Y. (2008, November 10). Rural buzzwords in 30 years. *China Daily*.

Yan, Y. (2011). The individualization of the family in rural China. *Boundary 2, 38*(1), 203–229.

Zhang, H. (2007). China's new rural daughters coming of age: Downsizing the family and firing up cash-earning power in the new economy. *Signs, 32*(3), 671–698.

Zhang, J., Zhang, L., Rozelle, S., & Boucher, S. (2006). Self-employment with Chinese characteristics: The forgotten engine of rural China's growth. *Contemporary Economic Policy, 24*(3), 446–458.

Zhang, L. (2001). *Strangers in the city: Reconfigurations of space, power, and social networks within China's floating population*. Stanford, CA: Stanford University Press.

Zhang, L., de Brauw, A., & Rozelle, S. (2004). China's rural labor market development and its gender implications. *China Economic Review, 15*(2), 230–247.

Zhao, L. T. (2004). *Path to private entrepreneurship: Markets and occupational mobility in rural China*. Unpublished doctoral dissertation, Stanford University, Stanford, U.S.

2 The peasant question and the gender question

The peasant question has been a key issue in China's modernization (Jacka & Sargeson, 2011, p. 4; Qin, 2003, p. 139). The state has initiated various campaigns and policies to modernize agriculture and to transform the rural economy, starting from the revolutionary land reform to destroy the feudalist legacy after 1949, to the establishment of the communes and the collective economy in the 1950s, to the redistribution of land to individual households since 1978. Still, rurality is frequently problematized in a teleological discourse of modernization theories, and the countryside has often been regarded as a brake on the nation's modernization by policy makers (Wen, 2001). In the recent decades, the state has relied on the liberalization of markets to reform the countryside, with massive labor redistribution from labor-saturated agriculture to other economic sectors. Some studies have focused on how rural laborers are absorbed into cities and factories under the diffusion of cultural and economic resources, being empowered and exploited (Fan, 2003, 2004; Lee, 1995; Pun, 2005); others have turned to the communities and groups that have been "left behind" by the massive migration, industrialization, and urbanization processes (Ye & Wu, 2008). The framework can be traced to the dichotomy between modern urban cores and traditional rural peripheries in modernization theories (Murphy, 2002).

Similar to the stigmatization of the "rurality," rural women have been represented as a burdensome, backward, vulnerable, and risk-averse group in a large body of literature. Under the "state patriarchy," peasants and rural women in particular are expected to transform themselves into instrumental agents of development and to transform the countryside from a brake on modernization to a "driving force" of the national economy (Jacka & Sargeson, 2011; Stacey, 1983; Zhang, 1999). However, their entrepreneurial mentalities and activities are often portrayed as deviating from their rurality or femininity, and development per se often introduces new forms of exploitation and self-exploitation in the growing rural-urban inequalities.

This chapter begins with a discussion of peasants and their economic choices, and then moves on to the gender question in contemporary rural China. Understanding these two questions helps to shed light on rural men's and women's preferences of employment, and how they are negotiated in the family. Finally, the theoretical discussion is extended to various development models in Chinese villages, in which personal choices and family strategies evolve together with the restructuring of the rural economy.

Rational peasants or passive peasants

Peasants or smallholding villagers have been the target of theoretical debates in agrarian reforms and rural changes. Such theories have studied how small agrarian producers existed in the capitalized economy (Jacobs, 2010). Those from the modernization perspective were manifested in micro-level studies in neoclassical literature, by assuming rational individuals with cost-benefit calculations to make decisions of working in different regions and economic sectors (Murphy, 2002). Modernization, then, is a process of diffusing resources from urban cores to rural peripheries, and of moving labor from traditional to modern economic sectors. Historically, the resource and labor flows had been channeled through the hierarchical networks of Chinese villages around urban centers and market towns, which was more complicated than the simple dichotomy (Skinner, 1964, 1965).

The rationality of peasants has been questioned historically. Huang (1990) suggests that traditional Chinese peasants followed a safety-first logic and kept investing cheap family labor into labor-intensive agriculture and handicrafts despite declining labor returns. Peasants' survival strategy contributed to a process of "involution" even in the commercialization of the rural economy, which did not give rise to utility-maximization logic. This was in line with the populist tradition with an emphasis on the "labor-consumer balance." According to Chayanov, the labor–consumer balance is closely related to a cyclical socio-economic differentiation based on demographic structures of households, rather than class status in production and accumulation (Chayanov, 1989; Jacobs, 2010). Following the populist theorization, studies found that peasants did not prioritize the goal of profit maximization but norms of kinship and reciprocity (Sahlins, 1974) and village solidarity (Scott, 1985). As suggested by the notion of "moral economy" (Scott, 1976), the security of collective sharing and reciprocity remained important for peasants. In subsistence economies, the family and the collective support their members against starvation regardless of their economic contribution (Chayanov, 1989), so as to survive even through impoverishment.

Rationality of peasants was still rediscovered in some studies about their sophisticated calculations about the returns from different labor investments (Brandt, 1989; Rawski, 1989). Rather than assuming the corporate villages as protecting poor peasants and leveling income inequality, Samuel Popkin (1979) suggested that peasants were eager to innovate based on a calculated assessment, and market expansion and commercialization did not necessarily harm the welfare of peasants but could serve the interests of profit-maximizing individuals. But to Marxist theorists, peasants were neither liberated by market forces nor protected by corporate communities. Instead, peasants had faced oppressive landlords, and then the more relentless market forces. With the incorporation of the peasant economy in the Western world within the capitalist economy, the peasants faced new and unfamiliar forces that locked them into a market economy (Kautsky, 1988 [1899]). Different from the rational peasant approach that focuses on free market competition in the pursuit of economic efficiency, the Marxist approach sees peasants as exploited both by landlords and by the market.

All the camps can find support from recent changes in China. For modernization theories, the liberalization of prices and the dismantling of communes were a stimulus to both agricultural productivity and villagers' mobility in the labor market beyond their community. For the populist school, market reforms also brought back elements of the traditional peasant production, such as the features of smallholder households and the kinship basis of economic life. Peasants might move for the unequal opportunities in different areas and economic sectors, but often in a "circulation" pattern that migrants regularly return home to help with farming and to follow the demographic cycles of getting married, having children, recovering from sickness, or spending the rest of life. Meanwhile, such trends also speak to Marxist theories about class differentiation rather than demographic differentiation. In most cases, peasants remained rural-based and moved back and forth to generate wealth for the cores and reproduce themselves in the peripheries (Murphy, 2002), because either side provides insufficient support for income and welfare. This created a group of "quasi-" or "half-" workers in the industrial world as a result of unfinished proletarianization (Pun & Lu, 2010), which reflected structural inequalities in parallel with the rising opportunity structures. Instead of seeing peasants' choices as only to satisfy basic needs or to calculate labor returns, their behaviors are shaped by relations with capitalist forces.

China provided a unique setting with regard to the changing preferences and the structural constraints faced by peasants. First, regarding the agriculture/industry dichotomy, peasants were first excluded from and then widely utilized as cheap laborers in nonagricultural sectors. Throughout the Maoist era, the socialist developments assumed the supremacy of industries and prioritized urban development at the expense of peasants' mobility. Modeled after the Soviet Union, China leveled the political status of poor peasants as part of the revolutionary class like the industrial proletariat, but in economic terms, peasants were constrained in passive and immobile positions. Peasants were excluded from industrial and commercial economies, and denied access to more prestigious urban jobs.

As such, the target of market liberation was not traditional peasants but those in the socialist urban-rural job hierarchies. Even when rural industries were first allowed, they were largely developed on a collective basis so as to supplement the urban state-owned industrial sectors. Such job hierarchies remained influential to some extent and were gradually restructured by the market economy when the state loosened the previous rigid control of labor mobility across the rural-urban divide and allowed local variations in regulations on land use and economic activities. As the institutional barriers were gradually removed for peasants to run sidelines, rural industries, and private businesses, it became the individual's responsibility to transition from the underutilized labor force to compete and exert market rationality, and those who failed to be absorbed into modern economic sectors became the "left-behind." As such, the urban-rural dichotomy was to some extent replaced by the divide of migrants and the left-behind, but such dichotomies often underestimate the linkage between rural internal dynamics and labor influx into cities. In fact, most peasant households did not leave their land completely and continued multiple job-holding practices (Van der Ploeg & Ye, 2010), despite the concentration and polarization of industrial capital.

Second, concerning the community/market dichotomy, Chinese rural communities have been shaped by both socialist and traditional legacies and continued to play a role under the market reform. The socialist state had tried to eliminate the feudalist communal and lineage controls but had compromised and retained its elements in establishing the collective farming system. Some developmental policies, such as the rural-urban divide, have created material conditions conducive to traditional family ties (Davis & Harrel, 1993), because people were tied to land and the local community and not allowed to move freely. Under the urban-rural divide, peasants were earthbound as a sign of devotion to collective farming rather than the traditional "safety first" logic. This was to serve the massive increase of labor input and to enhance the total agricultural output, while ignoring the declining marginal labor return (Huang, 1990). Modernization theories have seen the market to be the solution to remove institutional barriers and liberalize peasants from communities, but the market reform has also witnessed the revival of kinship and communal networks. Furthermore, collective ownership remained dominant in the rural land system despite household land tenures, and family farms relied on their attachment to the rural collective to gain the land use rights.

Interestingly, some studies found that the community was able to achieve economic goals, such as in some cases of rural industrialization. Huang (1990) found that commercialization per se did not increase the marginal value of agricultural work, but the growth in rural industry effectively diverted labor away from agriculture. Different from the traditional "break-even" communities, the corporate structures of the villages act like a company oriented toward market efficiency in a form of local state corporatism (Oi, 1992, 1999). The local state mobilized local populaces, whose reciprocity and loyalty contributed to the development of township and village enterprises (TVEs) in the 1980s in Sunan (southern Jiangsu Province) (Wei, 2004, 2010). In the 1990s, the Sunan model was revised due to the privatization of TVEs, but the community continued to play a role in the provision of social insurance and collective infrastructure, although the community weakened its control over the local resource and labor allocation and peasants enjoyed fewer of the "insider" benefits. In short, the market/community dichotomy in China is complicated by the capitalist forces and the socialist legacy, including localized economic incentives and regulations and various forms of the household economy. These forces shape not only the preferences of peasants but also how they are selected into new economic sectors, and how household choices are mixed with individual career pursuits and communal goals, leading some to be still "locked" in the farming sector, whereas others opt for other opportunities, and some move back and forth between different economic sectors.

Peasants have often been described as passive, immobile, and conservative as a base for the traditional social order compared with the "progressive" force of industrial proletariats, as in some Marxist theories. In contemporary China, peasants have frequently moved across the industry/agriculture and community/ market dichotomies. In different moments of market reforms, peasants were sometimes praised as the driving force of economic development, but were still often portrayed as vulnerable and of "low quality." Not only does peasant production remain related to kinship and lineage elements, but more importantly, structural inequalities have been reproduced in the new job hierarchies. Such structural constraints and traditional norms need to be studied by taking into account different human agencies exerted by peasants at the grassroots level. For example, peasants may adopt work patterns that could be read as self-exploitation but also contain elements of innovation and competitiveness.

Built on the rational peasant and agrarian change debates, this book does not take peasants simply as preferring secure or risky investments or as conservative or revolutionary production forces: their choices are contextualized and time-varying. Rather than seeing peasants as an essentialist and homogeneous category, Marxist theories focus on class differentiation, and the populist school emphasizes demographic and cyclical differentiation. They have paid insufficient attention to gender differentiation, however, because they either assume that gender inequality can be explained in class terms or use household labor as the main component in smallholder economies rather than gendered labor (Jacobs, 2010). In China, the Marxist agenda of gender equalization had encountered difficulties, and women were again questioned to be "losing out" or "left behind" with discussions of their merits and positions in different economic sectors and jobs. These processes are not only merit-based but also power-laden, closely interwoven with family and gender dynamics. In a time when the production responsibility system has been reinstated for three decades and the rural economy has been highly decentralized, family and gender dynamics are particularly important in understanding the new dynamics of labor allocation and resource distribution.

Strong women or left-behind women

Under the influence of Marxist theories, the socialist regime in China promoted gender equalization programs that assumed that men and women could do the same kind of work, and women could only be empowered via their engagement in paid work outside home. Despite the promotion of ideal women as strong and capable workers, the sharing of household responsibilities was never part of the Marxist ideology (Bian, 1987; Blau & Ferber, 1986, p. 335; Wang & Li, 1982). In rural areas, women were brought into the collective farming system. However, the official emphasis on gender sameness and paid work was less well implemented in rural areas than in cities. Despite the official appraisal of women labor models and the "iron girls" (*tieguniang*) for their virtues of "eating bitterness" (*chiku*) to overcome their biological obstacles (Honig, 2000), the gendered principle of work organization remained for the majority of women. Rural women frequently worked cross the farming and family boundary, and many rural collectives tended to assign the perceived "light" tasks to women and give them fewer work points. In some cases, the increase in women's labor force participation was closely related to the change in gender role attitudes toward individualistic-egalitarian values, whereas in others, the extra-familial work of women and gender role attitudes did not evolve together (Haller & Hoellinger, 1994).

China's market reform has given rise to a celebration of the triumph of human capital over redistributive power (Nee, 1996).[1] Under the market-oriented reform, the state withdrew its overall control from people's daily lives, and the socialist ideology of gender equality, such as summed up by Mao's statements that "women hold up half the sky" and "anything a man can do a woman can also do" (Hershatter, 2007), has been less influential. As the regime's previous commitment to gender equality has given way to policy repertoires that prioritize economic development, the socialist ideology of gender sameness was widely criticized when the public reemphasized "gender differences" in the market economy starting in the 1980s (Honig, 2000). When the state is no longer imposing a uniform ideology of gender equality, people are allowed to voice their diverse choices based on different gender role attitudes and education levels (Shu, 2004). Despite greater job mobility for both sexes, gender differences have been enhanced, given the lack of family-friendly policies (Blau & Ferber, 1986). Although female labor participation rates remain high when there is a market demand (Hu, 2008, p. 32), married women are less likely than men to change jobs for career advancement but more likely to change jobs for family reasons or quit the labor market (Cao & Hu, 2007).

The gender gap in employment has varied across different economic sectors, such as in the state-owned enterprises, the collective sector, and the private sector. As the expanding labor markets are more competitive with limited economic security and public child care assistance, women are confronted with greater tension between work and family (Hu, 2008). Related to this, education benefits women more in the state sector and less so in the rural collective sector, and women's education counted even less compared with that of men in the private sector (Parish, Zhe, & Li, 1995). In many economic sectors, not only workers have new freedom under market transition, employers also enjoy "growing freedom in labor management and their discriminatory tendencies rooted in traditional gender beliefs" (Cao & Hu, 2007, p. 1555).

As such, rural women have been doubly marginalized for their rural status and female identity. Urban working women typically have a paid job outside home coupled with welfare and pension. In the countryside, despite a broadened external market with the removal of institutional barriers, there are fewer regulations against the traditional gender beliefs in farm work or migrant work. Rural women usually cannot get permanent and stable jobs in cities, and the return from collective farming to family farms has made women more family oriented. In the early reform years, men were often the first ones to leave the village to work at urban construction sites (Unger, 1985, p. 598); women were often denied opportunities to participate in the wage sector and were relegated to farm work (Gao, 1994), often by blending fieldwork in combination with other domestic responsibilities (Judd, 1990). In some studies, only one third of migrant labor was estimated to be female, and out of them, only one third were married women (Tan, 2004). But as the reform has unfolded, both men and women have become less earthbound over time, and the farming tasks are likely to be taken by middle aged women than young women (de Brauw et al., 2008). Young people are more active in migrant work than older generations, and among them, the proportion of women tends to be higher. Women count for almost half of migrant workers in the age group of 16–20, but the proportion is reduced to around 25 percent at the age of 40 (Department of Household Surveys, National Bureau of Statistics of China, 2011). Many young couples migrate together, as both spouses are migrant workers, but they often leave their children at the place of origin (ibid). In general, women's employment is still very responsive to the presence of grandparents and young children in the household (Song & Logan, 2010).

Related to the disadvantages of women in the market, social media has moved from the socialist appraisal of iron girls and gender sameness to another extreme, seeing women as a "vulnerable" group and a "left-behind" category. Women were often seen as an underutilized population in the modernization campaign, and their "low quality" and risk-averse character were formulated to be related to limited productivity (China Women's News, 2006; Jacka & Sargeson, 2011; Zhong & Di, 2005). Governments and state organizations proposed to transform women into an instrumental group in rural development, by raising women's "quality," just as in the "two studies, two competitions" (*shuangxue shuangbi*) program organized by the Women's Federation (Judd, 2002). Rather than following the Maoist "gender sameness" ideology, the new approaches emphasize self-development in achieving market efficiency, without challenging structural gender inequalities directly. Moreover, market success is measured by the visibility and remuneration of women's work in income-generating work, which is related to an achievement-based and entrepreneurial mentality, or individual "qualities."

Such measurements reflect the rediscovery of the gendered capabilities under the rising neoliberal ethos but overlook women's capability and agency in a great variety of economic activities, such as in the domestic or "left-behind" spheres. In the restructuring of the rural (as well as urban) economy, job categories could be informal, vague, and under transformation. Rural people have been observed to be moving back and forth between different economic sectors or hold multiple jobs, and such flexibility, frequently embraced by women, could be seen as self-exploitation or innovation depending on the nature of economic sectors.

For example, the farming sector has been devalued along with the trend of feminization of agriculture, which suggests a modified inside vs. outside boundary (Croll, 1983; Entwisle, Short, Zhai, & Ma, 2000). Farming, shifting from the collective to the household management system, was not a "public" form of employment but was redefined as "inside work" (Chen, 2004). Compared with other income-generating work, farming is often related to non-wage compensations that are difficult to be recognized as individual earning, and agricultural jobs often have flexible work schedules that are more compatible with family responsibilities. However, farming is still considered an important career and the fallback position for many peasants, and they have learned to switch between on-farm and off-farm work in an adaptive way. Furthermore, the nature of agriculture varies across regions, and men's and women's relations to farming need to be contextualized.

Another example was rural sideline production, which had been a marginalized but persisting segment in the collective farming system. Under the market reform, some sideline production remained to be an extension of home-based domestic work and categorized as "inside work," in which women's labor was heavily used. In other cases, it could be the basis of "specialized households" (*zhuanyehu*) that specialized in raising livestock, processing foodstuffs, or producing handicrafts, with a high proportion of commodity production in the expanding markets (Jacka, 1997). With regard to the further development of private sectors, studies have found the leading role of men in family businesses (Entwisle, Henderson, Short, Bouma, & Zhai, 1995) and the "takeover" of specialized household businesses previously run by women by their husbands when these businesses develop to a certain level (Jacka, 1997). In a great variety of ventures, women's roles are often vague and continuously negotiated, falling into home-based sideline production or the "courtyard economy" (Jacka, 1997). The actual roles played by women in the development of sidelines and private ventures need to be studied, either characterized by active participation or imbued with self-exploitation.

Similarly, the nascent rural industries had allowed many rural women to find local jobs without migration, but with the development and formalization of rural industries, women may face similar discrimination as in urban industries, particularly for professional and entrepreneurial positions. Given the rise of "male control" within and beyond the household economy (Judd, 1994, 2002), women's labor engagement was often underestimated and considered less than labor, filling in the left-behind positions and multitasking as required by the household economy (Song, 2015). As such, women's risk-averse character and vulnerability have been highlighted as the foundation of the new labor division that links achievement and competition with masculinity and passivity with femininity (Rofel, 1999). This book investigates how men and women negotiate work opportunities when such chances grow along with the evolvement of the farming sector, sideline activities, private business, and rural wage jobs, and whether new economic sectors are dominated by men or create room for women's participation.

Regarding the debate on whether and how women lose out in the market transition (Honig & Hershatter, 1988; Zuo, 2003), previous studies have focused on formal individual employment outcomes, such as the types and the quality of jobs (Matthews & Nee, 2000; Michelson & Parish, 2000) or the difference in earnings (Shu & Bian, 2003). This book adopts more flexible definitions of employment outcomes for men and women to examine the potential of creative, productive, and entrepreneurial activities in rural areas due to the lack of external and formal paid work in conventional terms. Rather than focusing on independent career development outside of the family, this book investigates how women and men move back and forth between different economic sectors, and how it is related with their respective capabilities and gendered obstacles. By taking into consideration finer categories of work, this book looks at how labor participation is negotiated between genders and across generations within and beyond households.

Individualization and householding

In reshuffling job hierarchies and gender roles, rural China is characterized by the resilient significance of the household in providing care and security. In contrast with urban welfare systems, rural people had to rely on their families for welfare support and economic security. The consequent subordination of individuals to the overall interest of the family, according to family economists, is justified by the maximization of household utility that is considered favorable to all family members (Becker, 1981). To family economists, gender is among the personal traits that contribute to the rational division of labor. It may be wise for women to specialize in the domestic sphere and for men to specialize in paid work, based on their cumulated capabilities (Becker, 1981).

Other studies, however, found that gender employment patterns cannot be reduced to economics but are deeply rooted in the social expectations on gender roles. The family division of labor has been influenced by socially defined roles of husbands and wives and their relationships (Szybillo & Sosanie, 1977; White & Klein, 2002),[2] and the family-work conflict works differently for men and women and contributes to gender disparities in labor market outcomes (Zhang, Han, Liu, & Zhao, 2008). The presence of children in the household has been an important factor that interrupts married women's employment, and the high birth rates have confined women to the domestic sphere (Cohen & Bianchi, 1999; Yi & Chien, 2002).

As such, there have been different readings for the relationship between household and individuals. At one extreme, family economists see the family as the rational actor by assuming that what is the best for the family is also best for individuals, just as the moral economy school sees the communal welfare as important for taking care of peasants. At the other extreme, power relations continued to shape the family division of labor, such as the inside-outside divide, and individualization meant liberating individuals from the family constraints. This can be related with the May Fourth Movement tradition of women's emancipation in China, and looms large again under the influence of global capitalism and urban culture.

The market transition theory has provided a positive picture about labor mobility patterns for individuals with talent and expertise through bargaining and voluntary job changes (Nee & Cao, 2005). As such, the traditional division of family labor is subject to revisions when women grow more educated, skilled, and knowledgeable. Many studies have pointed out the positive relationship between women's education and their labor force participation (Bielby & Bielby, 1992;

Desai & Waite, 1991; Drobnic, Blossfeld, & Rohwer, 1999; Sharda & Nangle, 1981). In China, some studies find that market opportunities have driven the growth of young women's earning power outside the home (Yan, 2006; Zhang, 2007).

The growth of "girl power" can be seen as resulting from the new opportunities to work and experience a different life (Yan, 2006, p. 117). Due to the cash-earning power of the "new rural daughters" (Zhang, 2007), the rise of individual agency speaks to the shifting power relations within the family via the triumph of conjugality and the waning of patriarchy (Yan, 2009). The discussion of individualization, however, is not really new, "as the party state had propagated the notion of 'untying' individuals from traditional gendered institutions". Socialist revolutions claimed to liberalize women from their "feudal" attachment to families to be egalitarian comrades of men, but the new direction in female employment suggests a shift from a collectivist to an individualistic ethics of rights, self-development, and personal satisfaction (Evans, 2010, p. 981; Yan, 2009). As the reform unfolded, young people gained greater control over family property and employment decisions (Yan, 2006), and between sexes, the gender gap in off-farm work has been narrowed in the younger generation (Zhang, de Brauw, & Rozelle, 2004). Given the transformation from collective economy toward more diversified, deregulated, and privatized economic activities, such findings echoed the shift from collectivist to individualist goals of personal satisfaction (Evans, 2010).

However, the shift away from collectivist goals could also mean an emphasis on family goals, and the withering of an official agenda toward gender equality may lead to women's greater responsiveness to family needs. The market-oriented economy may give rise to a "market-supported naturalization" of women's emotional attributes, which highlights the increasing significance of good motherhood (Evans, 2010) and sometimes makes women less attached to the work force (Zhang et al., 2008). In sum, women face the mixed trends of the rising "girl power" and the increasing importance of being virtuous "wives and mothers." While some women enjoy the freedom to pursue their independent careers and personal satisfaction, others may choose being a housewife as a lifestyle (Hu, 2008).

Furthermore, the importance of the rural family economy continued for young men and women who gained some autonomy in the market. Popkin (1979) gives reason to understand "rationality" beyond focusing narrowly on self-interested individuals, and China's market reform has brought back the household-based calculation of labor investment. By the notion of "peasant household individualism," Nee (1984) suggests that peasants may prefer household goals over individualistic and community goals if the household labor division is adequate as a production unit. Household individualism has been reinforced by the prevalent patrilineal inheritance of land and housing and patrilocal marriage practices. In China, land remains collectively owned and its use rights are handled by family farms, whose tenure stability is considered crucial to food security and social stability.[3] Most economic transactions to sell agricultural output, get loans, and negotiate for compensation in land expropriation have been conducted at the household level. Without their attachment to a household, young men and women have limited land use rights and financial support.

However, households could also work as the resource rather than a constraining force for individual men and women. Daughters-in-law often left their farming tasks to mothers-in-law when they had a wage job, or left domestic work to mothers-in-law when they farmed (Chen, 2004, p. 559). Chen (2005) indicates that the presence of the extended family, or even parents living next door, reduces the domestic workload for both spouses. In particular, the common practice of grandparenting (Short & Sun, 2004) greatly enables mothers' career investment, and the presence of grandparents in the household "significantly reduces a mother's involvement in childcare" (Chen, Short, & Entwisle, 2000, p. 571). Unlike the pre-revolutionary period when women's work was confined "inside" and daughters-in-law did most of the domestic work, the work arrangements today between sexes and generations are more flexible. Jacka observed young women working in the fields and relying on their mothers-in-law for household responsibilities and child care, and they often worked together with kin and neighbors "to thresh and grind the wheat" after the harvest (Jacka, 2012, p. 14). The kin networks are not constrained to the paternal side, and women's natal families also provided channels of financial, material, and emotional support.

In addition to the grandparents' effect, the children's effect is also ambiguous. The implementation of the one-child policy in 1979 fundamentally altered the demographic composition of the family and the number of young children a working-age woman may have. Under such circumstances, the burden of child-rearing per se is lighter, and child care may no longer be a typical female task. In most rural areas, two children were allowed only if the first was a girl (Greenhalgh & Li, 1995). This can allow women to have a lighter child care responsibility and to work continuously, but it may also make women invest more in children who are more precious (Fong, 2004). Meanwhile, the fewer number of children may facilitate the education investment in daughters, but the parental perceptions of abilities and appropriate roles for girls and boys and of labor market outcomes for their education still contribute to their different investment in sons and daughters (Hannum, Kong, & Zhang, 2009). In an era when women are no longer expected to work outside as a norm, some scholars anticipate the emergence of an "M-shaped female labor force participation pattern" in China, in which the female labor force participation rates rise and peak before marriage and childbearing, then "drop sharply and then rebound after children enter school" (Hu, 2008, pp. 30–31). Their retirement age, however, is more ambiguous due to job availabilities and grandparenting responsibilities. This disrupted employment pathway can have negative implications on career development but may also reflect an increase in choice and confidence among women to work "on and off" (Song, 2015). As such, men and women's labor participation is continuously negotiated rather than being a fixed choice, and the family economy is a contested territory characterized by complicated interactions between different norms and practical concerns.

Rather than using the conventional notion of "household" as a homogeneous decision-making entity, Jacka used Douglass' discussion of householding, a fluid process "shaped through power relations and characterized by varying patterns of contestation and co-operation between kin" (Douglass, 2006, p. 421; Jacka, 2012, p. 19). Instead of the dichotomy of migrants vs. the left-behind, the "householding" process includes the flexible division of labor between wage work, agriculture, and care work, which depends on sharing and cooperation (Jacka, 2012). Rather than seeing the "left-behind" family members as "abandoned" and "sacrificing," this book tries to avoid overemphasizing the prohibiting effect of women's family roles on their labor participation, by looking into multiple possibilities of how families coordinate individual employment choices.

Two extreme women's images have been highlighted in social media as well as in literature: the traditional caring and home-oriented women and the modern career-oriented women outside the home sphere (Sjoberg, 2010). Between these two extremities there is a continuum in between, ranging from a woman who has an economically established husband and can "afford" to be a housewife (Hu, 2008, p. 32) to a woman who is in harsh family economic situations and finds it necessary to work outside (Yi & Chien, 2002). As such, there were various values and ethics about work and family, and women's family roles and their labor engagement are not necessarily the opposites of a dichotomy. Regarding the shifting boundary and connections between the two spheres, flexibility could be of special value for family strategies in which men may take the lead or spouses may move to new economic sectors together.

As such, the "family adaptive strategy" (Moen & Wethington, 1992) may be a useful tool to link individual actions with social changes. Despite the celebration of individual freedom under the market reform, previous studies found that there is no simple causal relationship between female labor force participation and gender role attitudes (Haller & Hoellinger, 1994). In the fluid process of family cooperation, women can also adapt their roles flexibly, sometimes in line with the rising "girl power" and sometimes following the lead of virtuous wives and mothers. Given mixed trends in gender role attitudes and family norms, this book looks at both normative and economic concerns that help to shape the gendered division of labor within and beyond the household.

Local development contexts

Although employment seems to become a matter of "choice" in the market economy (Hu, 2008, p. 23), it is still embedded in the settings of economic development, gender norms, and welfare regimes (Fuwa, 2004). Previous studies have looked at the presence of the state and the market in shaping the countries' industrial structures, labor market conditions, work-related regulations and organization politics (Dex, 2004), and thus family employment patterns. Studies in Chinese villages have illustrated different development patterns in the countryside that have shaped different employment patterns of men and women. Such employment patterns are subject to the constraints related to men's and women's roles in the family and in society, and shaped by the influences of the central and the local state (Little, 1991).

Post-Mao development policies and open-up strategies have favored the eastern region, which benefited from its favorable geographic and economic conditions (Fan, 1997). Given the large and increasing income gap between eastern, central, and western regions (Cai, Wang, & Du, 2002), the differences between inland and coastal areas have interacted with those between the wheat region in the North and the rice region in the South (Buck, 1937) and those of the urban-rural gap in shaping labor flows within and across the localities. Even within the same region, the market expansion has different impacts, and many farm households fail to benefit from the market expansion due to their capacities and political-economic conditions (Su, 2009). Some have suffered more from the rising market inequalities, partly due to the local variations in land policies, property structures, and social institutions, as well as infrastructures that serve agriculture and other economic sectors.

Due to the withering away of interventionist government policies, local politics play a more important role in shaping developmental pathways. Local leaders may pass on autonomy to villagers, but some maintain and reorganize their regulative power. In either case, the improvement of local economic performance has often been used to evaluate the administrative capability of local officials (Su, 2009). To achieve economic efficiency, some villages have relied on the collective economy rather than embracing free markets. Under the collective coordination of the rural economy, the local office may have different takes on gender equality that contribute to the local employment patterns for men and women. For other, more laissez-faire villages, the local discretion in implementing government policies may also change the context in which men and women interpret economic opportunities and negotiate the family division of labor.

For example, Daqiu Village near the municipality of Tianjin in northern China had been a model of rural development based on collective ownership and management. It became famous in the 1980s when the village was transformed into a village corporation based on a cold-rolled steel mill. The corporation managed agricultural, industrial, service, and commercial enterprises in the village, but the industrialization did not bring equivalent job opportunities for men and women. According to the article about Daqiu in *Chinese Women* (*Zhongguo Funv*) reviewed by Jacka (1990), the majority of married women became housewives in the 1980s when industrial workers accounted for 96 percent of the local labor force, in contrast to the situation in the Maoist era when most women had participated in collective labor. This was said to be a natural outcome given the heavy and stressful work in industry by the busy husbands, who had high enough wages to support the family and needed the wives to support them as homemakers.

Such entrepreneurial dynamics reflected a new gender order that deviated from the socialist gender-equalization agenda. When the urban reforms witnessed the layoff of women to reduce "surplus" labor (Liu, 2007), Daqiu's case added to the wide discussion on whether "women returning home" was natural, inevitable, or beneficial in rural development. However, there were also other local development models that continued to incorporate women's labor participation, and there seems to be no simple relationship between development models and gender ideology.

In areas with different levels of industrialization, rural women were found to participate in running small-scale enterprises (Judd, 1994) and participated in sideline industries (Jacka, 1997), and such activities could reflect women's marginalized role as a cheap and flexible labor force as well as their advantages in these newly developed economic sectors. For areas in which family businesses have been prevalent, women could either be marginalized in the male-dominated businesses or play an important role in the development of the enterprises, although with no symbolic recognition of their roles (Goodman, 2004). Due to the mixed context of peasant economy, socialist legacy, patriarchal traditions, and market reforms, the collective coordination of the rural economy is not necessarily related to the Marxist agenda of women's liberation, and private accumulations can also work as resources for the empowerment of women. Their impacts on gender employment outcomes have to be examined in different atmospheres and mechanisms of cooperation and competition.

The official narrative has suggested that it is up to the process of building "women's quality" to define the ambiguous roles of women's labor participation, as suggested by the government-sponsored "two studies, two competitions" campaigns, which encouraged women to achieve economic success and to make "social contributions" (Judd, 2002). The central government has adopted a loose position to define gender relations in the labor market, and women are encouraged to join the market competition together with their male counterparts. Meanwhile, the public and the media began to abandon the ideology of gender sameness and to voice that women are different from men. The coexisting narratives have put more burdens on individual women to pursue self-development and balance multiple obligations. Such a dilemma is salient when local communities provide limited job opportunities and villagers rely on themselves to seek migrant work based on their individual talents and experiences. The migration experience has empowered young women by adding to their cash-earning power, as Yan (2006) found in Heilongjiang in northern China and Zhang (2007) found in Hubei in central China. However, they face new market hierarchies, such as that of "cultured" and "uncultured" (Jacka, 2005) and that of nearby and remote villages from urban centers. Rather than focusing on individual qualities, this book examines changes in opportunity structures and resource constraints in shaping employment patterns.

This book shares with previous studies the research interest about the extent to which men and women have benefited from the process of China's economic reform regarding their positions in the labor market. But this book contextualizes their choices and strategies in different developmental contexts that are shaped by the "diffusely present" state and the different patterns of urbanization and industrialization. It adds to the existing findings that women are multiply disadvantaged in the market economy, and explores their new adapting strategies to take advantage of economic opportunities in creative ways. Furthermore, this book looks at both men and women who are partners and competitors in negotiating their individual and family goals. Their employment experiences are cohort-specific in different stages of industrialization and urbanization processes, and change over the life course given changing individual and family goals.

Notes

1   Some analysts emphasize the increasing returns to human capital in an increasingly market-oriented economy (Nee, 1989, 1996; Nee & Cao, 2005), but others find the continuing significance of political capital in China as a post-socialist society (Bian & Logan, 1996; Walder, 1996). In particular, political capital and redistributive power (such as wielded by a Communist Party member or cadre) is still rewarded in various ways, including via the new opportunities for rent seeking and profit making provided by economic reform (Walder, 2003). But the related gender dimension needs to be further elaborated and incorporated.
2   Built on different gender role attitudes, families can be categorized into traditional ones (the wife is responsible for the traditional feminine tasks, while her husband is responsible for providing the family with status and income), egalitarian ones (married women are allowed the opportunity for equal achievement and advancement), and neo-traditional ones (the husband and the wife freely assist each other with the traditionally sex-determined family obligations) (Poloma & Garland, 1971).
3   Although Marxist theories have seen peasants as petty commodity producers in relation to capitalist forces with limited focus on the internal organization of the household, in many societies, expanding capitalism did not make family farms dissolve (Kautsky, [1899]1988). Post-socialist China provides another case that rural changes are not advancing "toward the same end" of modern managerial farming.

References

Becker, G. (1981). *A treatise on the family*. Cambridge, MA: Harvard University Press.
Bian, Y. J. (1987). A preliminary analysis of the basic features of the life styles of China's single-child families. *Social Sciences in China, 8*, 189–209.
Bian, Y. J., & Logan, J. R. (1996). Market transition and the persistence of power: The changing stratification system in urban China. *American Sociological Review, 61*(5), 739–758.
Bielby, W. T., & Bielby, D. B. (1992). I will follow him: Family ties, gender-role beliefs, and reluctance to relocate for a better Job. *American Journal of Sociology, 97*, 1241–1267.
Blau, F. D., & Ferber, M. A. (1986). *The economics of women, men, and work*. Englewood Cliffs, NJ: Prentice-Hall.
Brandt, L. (1989). *Commercialization and agricultural development: Central and eastern China, 1870–1937*. Cambridge: Cambridge University Press.
Buck, J. (1937). *Land utilization in China*. Chicago: University of Chicago Press.
Cai, F., Wang, D. W., & Du, Y. (2002). Regional disparity and economic growth in China: The impact of labor market distortions. *China Economic Review, 13*, 197–212.
Cao, Y., & Hu, C. Y. (2007). Gender and job mobility in postsocialist China: A longitudinal study of job changes in six coastal cities. *Social Forces, 85*(4), 1535–1560.
Chayanov, A. V. (1989). *Theory of peasant economy*. Manchester: Manchester University Press.

Chen, F. N. (2004). The division of labor between generations of women in rural China. *Social Science Research, 33,* 557–580.

Chen, F. N. (2005). Employment transitions and the household division of labor in China. *Social Forces, 84*(2), 831–851.

Chen, F. N., Short, S. E., & Entwisle, B. (2000). The impact of grandparental proximity on maternal childcare in China. *The Population Research and Policy Review, 19,* 571–590.

China Women's News. (2006). *Restrictions and solutions: New socialist countryside construction and women's development.* Retrieved March 1, 2017, from http://www.womenofchina.cn/womenofchina/html1/features/politics/8/4234-1.htm

Cohen, P. N., & Bianchi, S. M. (1999). Marriage, children, and women's employment: What do we know? *Monthly Labor Review, 122*(12), 22–31.

Croll, E. J. (1983). *Chinese women since Mao.* New York: Zed.

Davis, D., & Harrell, S. (1993). *Chinese families in the post-Mao era.* Berkeley: University of California Press.

de Brauw, A., Li, Q., Liu, C., Rozelle, S., & Zhang, L. (2008). Feminization of agriculture in China? Myths surrounding women's participation in farming. *The China Quarterly, 194,* 327–348.

Department of Household Surveys, National Bureau of Statistics of China (Guojia tongjiju zhuhudiaochabangongshi). (2011). *Xinshengdai nongmingong de shuliang jiegou he tedian (The new generation of rural migrant workers: Numbers, structures and characteristics).* Retrieved October 5, 2016, from www.stats.gov.cn/ztjc/ztfx/fxbg/201103/t20110310_16148.html

Desai, S., & Waite, L. J. (1991). Women's employment during pregnancy and after the first birth: Occupational characteristics and work commitment. *American Sociological Review, 56,* 551–566.

Dex, S. (2004). Work and families. In J. Scott, J. Treas, & M. Richards (Eds.), *The Blackwell companion to the sociology of families* (pp.435–456). Oxford: Blackwell Publishing Ltd.

Douglass, M. (2006). Global householding in Pacific Asia. *International Development Planning Review, 28*(4), 421–446.

Drobnic, S., Blossfeld, H. P., & Rohwer, G. (1999). Dynamics of women's employment patterns over the family life course: A comparison of the United States and Germany. *Journal of Marriage and the Family, 61*(1), 133–146.

Entwisle, B., Henderson, G. E., Short, S. E., Bouma, J. E., & Zhai, F. Y. (1995). Gender and family businesses in rural China. *American Sociological Review, 60,* 36–57.

Entwisle, B., Short, S. E., Zhai, F. Y., & Ma, L. M. (2000). Household economies in transitional times. In B. Entwisle & G. E. Henderson (Eds.), *Re-drawing boundaries: Work, household, and gender in China* (pp. 261–283). Berkeley: University of California Press.

Evans, H. (2010). The gender of communication: Changing expectations of mothers and daughters in urban China. *The China Quarterly, 204,* 980–1000.

Fan, C. C. (1997). Uneven development and beyond: Regional development theory in post-Mao China. *International Journal of Urban and Regional Research, 21*(4), 620–639.

Fan, C. C. (2003). Rural-urban migration and gender division of labor in transitional China. *International Journal of Urban and Regional Research, 27*(1), 24–47.

Fan, C. C. (2004). The state, the migrant labor regime, and maiden workers in China. *Political Geography, 23*(3), 283–305.

Fong, V. L. (2004). *Only hope: Coming of age under China's one-child policy.* Stanford, CA: Stanford University Press.

Fuwa, M. (2004). Macro-level gender inequality and the division of household labor in 22 countries. *American Sociological Review, 69*(6), 751–767.

Gao, X. X. (1994). China's modernization and changes in the social status of rural women. Translated by S. Katherine Campbell. In C. K. Gilmartin, G. Hershatter, L. Rofel, & T. White (Eds.), *Engendering China: Women, culture, and the state* (pp. 80–97). Cambridge, MA: Harvard University Press.

Goodman, D. S. G. (2004). Why women count: Chinese women and the leadership of reform. In A. McLaren (Ed.), *Chinese women – living and working* (pp. 19–41). London and New York: Routledge.

Greenhalgh, S., & Li, J. (1995). Engendering reproductive policy and practice in peasant China: For a feminist demography of reproduction. *Signs, 20*(3), 601–641.

Haller, M., & Hoellinger, F. (1994). Female employment and the change of gender roles: The conflictual relationship between participation and attitudes in international comparison. *International Sociology, 9*(1), 87–112.

Hannum, E., Kong, P., & Zhang, Y. P. (2009). Family sources of educational gender inequality in rural China: A critical assessment. *International Journal of Educational Development, 29,* 474–486.

Hershatter, G. (2007). *Women in China's long twentieth century.* Berkeley: University of California Press.

Honig, E. (2000). Iron girls revisited: Gender and the politics of work in the cultural revolution, 1966–76. In B. Entwisle & G. Henderson (Eds.), *Re-drawing boundaries: Work, households, and gender in China* (pp. 97–110). Berkeley: University of California Press.

Honig, E., & Hershatter, G. (1988). *Personal voices: Chinese women in the 1980s.* Stanford, CA: Stanford University Press.

Hu, C. Y. (2008). *A longitudinal study of married women's probability of being housewives in reforming urban China.* Unpublished doctoral dissertation, Department of Sociology, Louisiana State University, Baton Rouge, U.S.

Huang, P. C. (1990). *The peasant family and rural development in the Yangzi Delta, 1350–1988* (p. 421). Stanford, CA: Stanford University Press.

Jacka, T. (1990). Back to the wok: Women and employment in Chinese industry in the 1980s. *The Australian Journal of Chinese Affairs, 24,* 1–23.

Jacka, T. (1997). *Women's work in rural China: Change and continuity in an era of reform.* Cambridge: Cambridge University Press.

Jacka, T. (2005). *Rural women in urban China: Gender, migration, and social change.* Armonk, NY: M.E. Sharpe.

Jacka, T. (2012). Migration, householding and the well-being of left-behind women in rural Ningxia. *China Journal, 67,* 1–22.

Jacka, T., & Sargeson, S. (Eds.). (2011). *Women, gender and rural development in China.* Northampton, MA: Edward Elgar Publishing.

Jacobs, J. (2010). *Gender and agrarian reforms.* London and New York: Routledge.

Judd, E. R. (1990). Alternative development strategies for women in rural China. *Development and Change, 21*(1), 23–42.

Judd, E. R. (1994). *Gender and power in rural north China.* Stanford, CA: Stanford University Press.

Judd, E. R. (2002). *The Chinese women's movement between state and market.* Stanford, CA: Stanford University Press.

Kautsky, K. ([1899] 1988). *The agrarian question*. Winchester, MA: Zwan Publications.

Lee, C. K. (1995). Engendering the worlds of labor: Women workers, labor markets, and production politics in the south China economic miracle. *American Sociological Review, 60*(3), 378–397.

Little, J. (1991). Theoretical issues of women's nonagricultural employment in rural areas, with illustrations from the U.K. *Journal of Rural Studies, 7*(1–2), 99–105.

Liu, J. (2007). *Gender and work in urban China: Women workers of the unlucky generation*. London and New York: Routledge.

Matthews, R., & Nee, V. (2000). Gender inequality and economic growth in rural China. *Social Science Research, 29*(4), 606–632.

Michelson, E., & Parish, W. L. (2000). Gender differentials in economic success: Rural China in 1991. In B. Entwisle & G. Henderson (Eds.), *Redrawing boundaries: Gender, households, and work in China* (pp. 134–156). Berkeley: University of California Press.

Moen, P., & Wethington, E. (1992). The concept of family adaptive strategies. *Annual Review of Sociology, 18*, 233–251.

Murphy, R. (2002). *How migrant labor is changing rural China*. Cambridge: Cambridge University Press.

Nee, V. (1984). Peasant household individualism. *International Journal of Sociology, 14*(4), 50–76.

Nee, V. (1989). A theory of market transition: From redistribution to markets in state socialism. *American Sociological Review, 54*(5), 663–681.

Nee, V. (1996). The emergence of a market society: Changing mechanisms of stratification in China. *American Journal of Sociology, 101*(4), 908–949.

Nee, V., & Cao, Y. (2005). Market transition and the firm: Institutional change and income inequality in urban China. *Management and Organization Review, 1*(1), 23–56.

Oi, J. C. (1992). Fiscal reform and the economic foundations of local state corporatism in China. *World Politics, 45*(1), 99–126.

Oi, J. C. (1999). *Rural China takes off: Institutional foundations of economic reform*. Berkeley: University of California Press.

Parish, W. L., Zhe, X., & Li, F. (1995). Nonfarm work and marketization of the Chinese countryside. *The China Quarterly, 143*, 697–730.

Poloma, M., & Garland, T. N. (1971). The married professional woman: A study in the tolerance of domestication. *Journal of Marriage and Family, 33*(3), 531–540.

Popkin, S. L. (1979). *The rational peasant: The political economy of rural society in Vietnam*. Berkeley: University of California Press.

Pun, N. (2005). *Made in China*. Durham, NC: Duke University Press.

Pun, N., & Lu, H. L. (2010). Unfinished proletarianization: Self, anger and class action of the second generation of peasant-workers in reform China. *Modern China, 36*(5), 493–519.

Qin, H. (2003). Dividing the big family assets. In C. H. Wang (Ed.), *One China, many paths* (pp. 128–159). London: Verso.

Rawski, T. G. (1989). *Economic growth in Prewar China*. Berkeley: University of California Press.

Rofel, L. (1999). *Other modernities: Gendered yearnings in China after socialism*. Berkeley: University of California Press.

Sahlins, M. (1974). *Stone age economics*. London: Tavistock.

Scott, J. C. (1976). *The moral economy of the peasant.* New Haven, CT: Yale University Press.

Scott, J. C. (1985). *Weapons of the weak: Everyday forms of peasant resistance.* New Haven, CT: Yale University Press.

Sharda, B. D., & Nangle, B. E. (1981). Marital effects on occupational attainment. *Journal of Family, 2,* 148–163.

Short, S. E., & Sun, R. J. (2004). Grandmothers, formal care, and educational advantage in China. *Research in Sociology of Education, 14,* 7–31.

Shu, X. L. (2004). Education and gender egalitarianism: The case of China. *Sociology of Education, 77*(4), 311–336.

Shu, X. L., & Bian, Y. J. (2003). Market transition and gender gap in earnings in urban China. *Social Forces, 81*(4), 1107–1145.

Sjoberg, O. (2010). Ambivalent attitudes, contradictory institutions: Ambivalence in gender-role attitudes in comparative perspective. *International Journal of Comparative Sociology, 51,* 33–57.

Skinner, W. G. (1964). Marketing and social structure in rural China, Part 1. *Journal of Asian Studies, 24*(1), 3–43.

Skinner, W. G. (1965). Marketing and social structure in rural China, Part 2. *Journal of Asian Studies, 24*(2), 195–228.

Song, J. (2015). Women and self-employment in post-socialist rural China: Side job, individual career or family venture. China Quarterly, *221,* 229–242.

Song, J., & Logan, J. (2010). Family and market: Nonagricultural employment in rural China. *Chinese Journal of Sociology, 30*(5), 142–163.

Stacey, J. (1983). *Patriarchy and socialist revolution in China.* Berkeley: University of California Press.

Su, M. Z. (2009). *China's rural development policy: Exploring the "new socialist countryside".* Boulder, CO: First Forum Press.

Szybillo, G. J., & Sosanie, A. (1977). Family decision making: Husband, wife and children. *Advances in Consumer Research, 4,* 46–49.

Tan, S. (2004). Jiating celue, haishi geren zizhu: Nongcun laodongli waichu juece moshi de xingbie fenxi (Family strategy or individual autonomy: A gendered analysis of decision making in rural labor outmigration). *Zhejiang Academic Journal (Zhejing xuekan), 5*(2004), 210–214.

Unger, J. (1985). The decollectivization of the Chinese countryside: A survey of twenty-eight villages. *Pacific Affairs, 58*(4), 585–606.

Van der Ploeg, J. D., & Ye, J. Z. (2010). Multiple job holding in rural villages and the Chinese road to development. *Journal of Peasant Studies, 37*(3), 513–530.

Walder, A. G. (1996). Markets and inequality in transitional economies: Toward testable theories. *American Journal of Sociology, 101*(4), 1060–1073.

Walder, A. G. (2003). Elite opportunity in transitional economies. American Sociological Review, *68*(6), 899–916.

Wang, Y. L., & Li, J. R. (1982). Urban worker's housework. *Social Sciences in China, 3,* 147–165.

Wei, Y.H.D. (2004). Trajectories of ownership transformation in China. *Eurasian Geography and Economics, 45,* 90–113.

Wei, Y.H.D. (2010). Beyond new regionalism, beyond global production networks: Remaking the Sunan model, China. *Environment and Planning C. Government and Policy, 28,* 72–96.

Wen, T. J. (2001). Centenary reflections on the 'three dimensional problem' of rural China. *Inter-Asia Culture Studies, 2*(2), 287–295.

White, J. M., & Klein, D. M. (2002). *Family theories.* Thousand Oaks, CA: Sage.

Yan, Y. (2006). Girl power: Young women and the waning of patriarchy in rural north China. *Ethnology, 45*(2), 105–124.

Yan, Y. (2009). *The individualization of Chinese society.* Oxford: Berg.

Ye, J., & Wu, H. (2008). *Qianmo duwu: Zhongguo nongcun liushou funv (Dancing solo: Women left behind in rural China).* Beijing: Social Sciences Academic Press.

Yi, C. C., & Chien, W. Y. (2002). The linkage between work and family: Female's employment patterns in three Chinese societies. *Journal of Comparative Family Studies, 33,* 451–474.

Zhang, H. (2007). China's new rural daughters coming of age: Downsizing the family and firing up cash-earning power in the new economy. *Signs, 32*(3), 671–698.

Zhang, J., Han, J., Liu, P. W., & Zhao, Y. (2008). Trends in the gender earnings differential in urban China, 1988–2004. *Industrial & Labor Relations Review, 61*(2), 224–243.

Zhang, L. X, de Brauw, A., & Rozelle, S. (2004). China's rural labor market development and its gender implications. *China Economic Review, 15,* 230–247.

Zhang, Z. H. (1999). Rural industrialization in China: From backyard furnaces to township and village enterprises. *East Asia, 17*(3), 61–87.

Zhong, Z. B., & Di, J. H. (2005). Tudi liuzhuan zhong funv de diwei yu quanyi (Women's status and rights in land transfers). In L. Tan & B. H. Liu (Eds.), *Zhongguo funv yanjiu shinian (Review on the Chinese women's studies in recent 10 years)* (pp. 424–432). Beijing: Social Sciences Academic Press.

Zuo, J. P. (2003). From revolutionary comrades to gendered partners – marital construction of breadwinning in post-Mao urban China. *Journal of Family Issues, 24,* 314–337.

3 Bei Village
Rural industries and private businesses

Bei is located near the city of Shaoxing in the northeast of the Zhejiang Province in southeastern China. It used to belong to Bridge County and was rezoned to a suburban district of the city, Lake District, in 2003, which was subsumed into an expanding urban district in 2013.[1] Even before the locality was subsumed into the great urban areas, the countryside had been highly industrialized. As one of the early industrialized villages in the area, Bei Village is 7 kilometers from the county seat and 11 kilometers from the city center, and villagers paid visits to urban centers quite frequently for shopping, entertainment, and business. The village had 456 households and 1,128 people in 2006[2] with nine villagers' groups (or teams), and among them, eight teams were mainly made up of indigenous villagers and one team was relocated from another village whose land was expropriated for dam construction. Ninety-nine percent of the villagers belong to the Han ethnic group, and the two biggest kinship groups has around 200 people each, but they are loosely organized under the same surnames.

Historically, Bei Village has a labor-intensive double cropping system due to the long growing seasons and ample rainfall. In addition to the rice-growing traditions, Bei Village is famous for its traditional sidelines such as wine making. Such sidelines had been suppressed in the Maoist era, but around the time of the redistribution of collective farms to individual households in 1982, traditional sidelines and rural industries began to prosper in the village. Collective industries mushroomed in the 1980s and were mostly privatized in the 1990s. Meanwhile, many factory employees became traders, retailers, entrepreneurs, or contractors. In Bei Village, both local wage work and self-employed jobs have been prevalent, and the "informal sectors" such as private business have been an important part in its industrialization process. In 2006, the annual income per capita had reached around 10,000 yuan for villagers,[3] higher than the average of 8,619 yuan in Shaoxing city for rural residents[4] and the provincial average of 7,335 yuan.[5] Rural industries not only provided wage jobs for villagers but also absorbed around 700 migrant workers from inland rural areas. Along with rural industrialization, some of the village's land had been gradually developed to serve the industrial and service sectors. Such land expropriation had been incremental in the 1980s and the 1990s, and the regulations on land use had been tightened to stabilize the amount of arable land. In 2003, the village was rezoned from Bridge County to Lake District, and most of its land was rented by the collective to the district government under the city's new planning strategy to build a greenbelt area surrounding the city.

The field visits were carried out in 2004, 2005, 2006, 2007, 2009, and 2010. The interviews were collected with 85 couples: for 48 couples, only the husband was interviewed; for 34 couples, only the wife was interviewed; for 3 couples, both the husband and the wife were interviewed. In total, there were 88 respondents, including 51 males and 37 females. The age of the wives ranged from 29 to 77 at the time of investigation, and the age of the husbands ranged from 28 to 88. Five of them were current cadres in the village and villagers' teams. Drawing on in-depth interviews and local archives, this chapter looks closely at employment trajectories in the context of the changing local economic structures.

Farming, side jobs, and multitasking

Bei Village is located in the plain area of northeastern Zhejiang province, crisscrossed by rivers and canals. As one of the traditional grain-growing areas, farming has been particularly labor intensive in Bei Village. Before the socialist revolutions, land was typically small plots and work was mostly done by hands and feet. The low ratio of land to population made it difficult for agriculture to accommodate all the rural labor, and various family sideline activities based on traditional skills such as wine making, crafts making, and fishing had been natural extensions of the local grain-growing economy.

As in other rural areas, family sideline activities were officially prohibited under collective policies in the Maoist era. Given the overall control of rural market transactions by the state and the collectives, people involved in commercial activities were regarded as "speculators" and could be attacked politically (Lardy, 1985, p. 50). With the primary goal to meet the collective quota delivery targets, the collective had mobilized laborers to restructure the village landscape for agricultural use from the 1950s to the 1970s, which led to an increase of land from 826 mu to 974 mu.[6] However, the land scarcity still intensified given the growing population, and the amount of land per capital decreased from 1.03 mu in 1962 to 0.85 mu in 1982.[7] At the time of land redistribution, peasants recalled that each of them was entitled to about 1 mu of land.[8] Suffering from poverty, peasants had not given up their attempts to make "extra money" even in the Maoist era. Some villagers had continued to be engaged in nighttime fishing or tailoring secretly, but the involved peasants would be severely punished if they were caught by official teams sent by local governments.

But the overall political environment was not always harsh. During the 1960s and the 1970s, the institutional barriers had been periodically loosened, and a few men were sent to urban factories by production teams as temporary workers. Such migration had to be organized by production teams with government permissions, but it was welcomed by urban factories because the employers could take advantage of the villagers' specific skills such as that of wine making and did not need to provide long-term welfare benefits to them. These temporary

migrant workers submitted part of their wage to their production teams as a substitute of their work points[9] that they should have earned on collective farms to
exchange for food supplies, and then they could bring home the remaining wage.
Such temporary migrants were mainly men, due to the male dominance in the
traditional wine-making industries.

Some other attempts were initiated by carpenters, construction workers, and
craftsmen who specialized in corrosion protection for wine containers. They were
often organized into collective working groups to move and work on a contract
basis, and enjoyed some autonomy with the nominal attachment to the collective economy. Similar working groups were organized to dig fish ponds and to
construct river banks, which added to private income of peasant households and
also contributed to the collective income.

These migrant jobs were typically "men's work" and usually not an option
for women. In parallel with a small group of men who had left their homes to
earn income outside the village, many women had made income from home-
based needlework since the 1960s, and they had to multitask in collective farming
and sideline activities at the same time. During the 1970s, sideline needlework
involved 60 percent of Bei village's local women.[10] This work consisted of sewing
cloth with designs specified by customers in urban manufacturing or sales centers. Yu, a 52-year-old woman when interviewed in 2005, was one of the women
who began to learn such skills at the end of the 1960s after she graduated from
middle school. She later developed close connections with urban agents and was
in charge of distributing needlework tasks among local women. She recalled:

> I started learning needlework at the age of 14. There were two instructors
> from the town to distribute the needlework tasks and to teach local women
> the skills. My home was the most convenient place (for transaction), and
> women came to me for blank pieces for products, and got paid for their
> completed products. I became the "flower representative" [*huadaibiao*], as
> we sewed all kinds of flowers with our needlework. We worked on it day and
> night. We had not had local factories yet, people just worked in the produc-
> tion team, and we spent all our spare time sewing.

A particular reason that women were ready to switch to such side jobs was
that female labor was intentionally devalued in a labor-intensive farming system. In Bei Village, women's highest work point was four, whereas men could
reach the full point of ten. Related with the land scarcity, women's labor was
expected to be partly absorbed in the domestic sphere. Though the socialist
regime embraced the ideology of gender equality by motivating rural women
into collective agricultural production, women's role remained to be evaluated by local norms and the patriarchal understanding of womanhood. Several
male and female respondents regarded such arrangements as "natural" because
women needed to go home early to cook and take care of children, and thus
their lower work points corresponded to their usually shorter working time on
the collective farms.

The underappreciation of women's labor in agriculture ironically contributed to their advantage in making extra money when the urban market centers were seeking cheap female labor with specific sewing skills under a flexible work arrangement. Such self-employment opportunities enhanced the earning capability of women but not for men, because needlework was regarded as "inappropriate" for men. As Cao (a 52-year-old woman when interviewed in 2010) recalled, "We girls sewed in our spare time when we did not farm, and the communes chose to ignore us. It was for private money, and we or our representatives transacted with city agents when they came to the village. We could earn four yuan per week, much more than agricultural income. Because of needlework, people realized that girls could earn extra cash for the family."

Although most of this income was allocated for family needs, the proceeds from the sales came to the women themselves first, and their economic contributions were well recognized by other family members. In the 1970s, many families freed their daughters from heavy farming tasks so that they could specialize in needlework. In this perspective, agriculture was to some extent masculinized, and women in needlework were regarded as the major source of cash income of the family and were exempted from most farming tasks except in busy seasons. Compared with women's needlework, the labor flow of men in temporary migrant work was much more limited. To some extent, the institutional barriers for men to move away from farming were more rigid, and it was much more tolerable for women to work at home on needlework, as they had not been taken seriously in the collective farming system. It could be seen as a temporary return to the traditional "men plowing, women weaving" mode of production, but at this time, inside work was no longer devalued. Instead, it provided a cherished chance of making cash income, as suggested by the local saying, "three hoes cannot make as much money as three needles (*sange chutou buru sange zhentou*)."

The collective farms were redistributed to individual households in 1982.[11] Before that, young women had been particularly flexible in switching between collective farming and home-based sideline activities, and since then, both men and women gained more autonomy to move out of agriculture. But such a transition was not complete at the beginning, because peasants were not supposed to abandon farming responsibilities; otherwise the land might be taken back by the village. As a result, villagers had fragmented their farm work time and blended it with other economic activities, particularly among women and old people who were expected to have less career aspirations.

Over time, the local office had tended to allow more flexible land use practices for practical concerns by dividing farms into those for self-consumption (self-consumption land, *kouliangtian*) and those responsible for fulfilling state grain-purchase quotas (responsibility land, *zerentian*). In 1996, the village began to allow villagers to give away their "responsibility land" and retain only their "self-consumption land."[12] Almost half of the village's land was circulated into the hands of individual managerial farmers, and many peasants felt liberated from the farming obligation of grain quotas. Furthermore, the village leadership had gotten the economic capacity to pay agriculture-related taxes and payments for villagers, given their growing budget along with the growth of local industries. Such burdens of agriculture extraction had been more unbearable in other areas, and under the official narrative of "social harmony," such burdens had decreased and were officially removed by the central government around 2005. Unlike the conventional divide between the quality laborers who were absorbed in modern economic sectors and the less able workers left behind in the farming sector, multitasking had been a common strategy given the rising local job opportunities.

The decline in farming investment and multitasking practices was parallel with the shrinking of farming land in the village. The village and the local governments had expropriated small pieces of land for the construction of factories, roads, local schools, and hospitals in the 1980s and the 1990s. Furthermore, residential use was also an important reason: part of the land was assigned as housing plots (*zhaijidi*) for villagers' self-built housing, and part was expropriated to construct a suburban commercial housing neighborhood in the 1990s. As a result, the amount of farming land in the village decreased to 957 mu in the 1990s, and to around 800 mu in 2001. The amount of arable land was stabilized at the level of 800 mu for some time due to the tightening of the regulations on land use.

In 2003, the locality was rezoned to be part of Lake District, and the majority of the farming land was included in the city's greenbelt area to grow trees. The peasant households whose land was expropriated were compensated at an annual rent equivalent to their loss in agricultural output (300 yuan per mu in 2003 and 600 yuan per mu in 2004, and still growing over time). The rezoning process put an end to the multitasking practices for many peasants who had worked across agricultural and nonagricultural sectors for a long time. For many peasants, the farming burden was largely reduced, and the remaining small plots of land continued to be held by individual households to grow crops or vegetables mainly for family consumption. Most people who continued to cultivate the remaining small plots of land were old people in the family who had spent their youths multitasking on- and off-farm, whereas the younger generations usually had limited or no experience with farming, regardless of their gender.

Local industrialization and wage jobs

Before local industries took off at the beginning of the 1980s, women had benefited more from the flexibility in working in home-based needlework despite the governments' political scrutiny. The popularity of women's home-based work, however, did not last long in the following rural industrialization because of the rise of other economic opportunities that were attractive for both men and women. Although needlework had been an important source of cash income in the 1970s, it was again devalued due to its feminized and flexible form[13] and lost attractiveness when more formal jobs became available. In the late 1970s and the 1980s, the village collective established several textile, wine-making, and construction factories, in which many young women became textile workers and men became wine-making or construction workers. The biggest factory was the electronic cord factory. It began with producing materials of electronic cords for a big factory in Shanghai in 1981 and recruited around 200 workers in the village, in which female workers concentrated in positions that required nimbleness and men in technical positions such as that of operating machines.

Men with prior "external" market exposure were more active in founding the nascent rural industries as leaders and technicians. But at the same time, the rising rural industries provided comparable opportunities for men and women to enter wage sectors. For women who had multitasked in farming and home-based sidelines, their new dream was to become factory workers. Because income from needlework was sidelined, it became rare for younger generations to conduct sideline needlework, and they sometimes became more represented in the local wage labor force than men. In the 1970s, the respective proportions of men and women in local wage work were 29 percent and 21 percent for the cohort of respondents born in the 1940s, and 50 percent and 40 percent for those born in the 1950s. In the 1980s, the gender gap was reversed to 33 percent and 50 percent for the first cohort, and 44 percent and 65 percent for the second cohort (Table 3.1). From this perspective, local work opportunities had increasingly favored women over time. The key difference between Bei Village and Daqiu Village (in which the local industrialization favored male rather than female laborers, see Jacka, 1990) was that Bei Village focused on developing "light" industry, which was suitable for women who were considered to be nimble and hardworking. For local wage work, the reversed gender gap was frequently observed in the sample for the younger cohorts and in the later historical periods, whereas for migrant work, male dominance had been very consistent, although migrant work had been less popular due to the rural industrialization process.

The emergence of local industries occurred around the same time as the reinstatement of the family farming system. Because the farming sector was still dominated by labor-intensive manual work rather than machinery operations, peasants continued to visit and cultivate their fields every day but with shorter time for each visit, and moved between family tasks and other jobs quite frequently. Because the rural factories were mostly within walking distance from their homes, workers used their spare time to maintain the family farm. As such, farming gradually changed from a formal outside job to a casual inside type of work, which was shouldered more by women due to the gendered expectation for men to concentrate on career development rather than taking care of casual tasks. As such, some women adopted a multitasking strategy where they worked three shifts – factory, farm, and home.

The rise of local wage work among women was parallel with the decline of home-based needlework. As young women were directed to more rewarding sectors (first needlework and then factory work), old women were more likely to multitask in the less valued farm work. The transition from side jobs to formal jobs did not apply to men, as they were not expected to do side jobs. The flexibility to move between formal and informal economic sectors had been the advantage of women in the Maoist era, and men's lack of such flexibility became less of a concern because of the opening up of the market and the removal of institutional barriers.

Along with the transition of most women from the flexible and self-administered needlework to factory wage jobs, the factory regimes had adopted flexible working schedules at the beginning to allow women to make the most out of their domestic work schedules. In the early 1980s, the electronic cord factory had relied heavily on female workers for the manual labor on the cord covers, and the workshops disseminated home-based manual tasks to women and allowed them to work at home. Yu, the workshop manager at that time, said that she was responsible for collecting these manual products from "home workshops," which was followed by machinery processing in the factory. Such home workshops had existed for years until they were replaced by machinery workshops to deal with the changes in the cord cover materials.

As such, there had been vague boundaries between home-based work and factory work, and the collective coordination of entrepreneurial dynamics had been interwoven with the private accumulations at the grassroots level. The take-off of local industries had partly relied on the personal savings of managers and employees. As a common practice, peasants needed to make a deposit to be recruited as workers, and the amount was determined by the "level" of the enterprise (whether it was a township or village enterprise, how big and profitable it was expected to be). In other words, the rural industries in Bei Village were developed based on the aggregated private savings under the collective patronage, which provided the "red hat" of collective enterprises for accessing favorable policy and transaction benefits.

The mixed nature of rural industries led to different preferences in recruiting workers. For example, the "wives of village cadres" were given priority for entering village enterprises. The second type of workers to be recruited consisted of those who could afford a certain amount of deposit to enter the enterprises. Yu recalled when it took a deposit of 1,500 yuan to get in township factories or 300 yuan into village enterprises in the early 1980s. Yu entered the village's electronic cord enterprise under a third favored category: those women who had only one child. As a young candidate to be a female cadre, Yu chose to have no more children after having one daughter. Choosing to have only one child indicated a kind of "sacrifice" to comply with the new family planning policy, and such a behavior was rewarded by the village leadership using its influence on the recruitment procedures in collective enterprises. As such, the recruitment process had been based either on practical concerns to bring in economic resources or on the discretion of local leadership according to political capital or organizational links. Later on, when local wage jobs were widely available, the village leadership adopted an egalitarian principle to make sure each household had at least one wage earner.

But as the reform unfolded, collective enterprises became more independent from the village collective in pursuing their profit orientation and efficient management. The official independence of these enterprises was achieved via several waves of privatization throughout the 1990s, and by 1999, all the local enterprises were officially privatized. As found in other studies, the industries were more likely to be taken over by "insiders," and previous managers often became private entrepreneurs (Li & Rozelle, 2003). Along with privatization, the enterprises enforced more disciplinary management systems as a strategy to deal with stiffening competition. With a bigger pool of rural workers from the locality and from elsewhere, even local workers could be easily replaced. In particular, women's employment was more likely to be interrupted by family responsibilities, and women might quit work when they had children or grandchildren or became ill and weak. This happened to Cao in 1996. She entered the village electronic cord enterprise when her first daughter was two years old in 1984, and she said:

> We were allowed to have a second child after eight years from the birth of the first child, but I felt too busy to have a second one. . . . Finally I had the second daughter, and it really overwhelmed me. . . . I took a rest after the birth, but the factory soon requested me to return to my position because the machine could not wait there. . . . But I finally quit after several years, because my body went wrong and I had to have a uterus surgery. I asked for a leave for 120 days so I could fully recover, but the factory could not wait that long. They assigned someone else to my previous position, and I could not return.

Parallel with the urban state sector layoffs under the call of "women return home (*nvren huijia*)" (Li, 1994), rural wage jobs became increasingly insecure for women. Cao was quite depressed by being replaced so easily, whereas her sister comforted her that "as long as you have the diligent hands to work, you can always find a job," based on a sober recognition of employment relationships as increasingly market-dominated. As Cao later did, many local workers, middle-aged or old women in particular, began to work for different enterprises on a part-time or temporary basis, because when there was a need to retreat from the labor market temporarily, they had to start the job search again.

Employment disruption also occurred due to changes in labor demand by private enterprises. In the mid-1990s, the electronic cord enterprise replaced the use of textile with plastic materials as cord covers, thus its need for female workers greatly decreased. In 2008, the electronic cord enterprise moved the major workshops to an industrial park in a nearby county, which further reduced the percentage of local people among workers. Some interviewees quit their jobs around this time, because "it was not convenient to commute." Unlike what the local state corporatism model (Oi, 1992) would predict, enterprises gradually escaped from their local connections and became independent market actors. Rural industries turned to hire more migrant workers from poor inland provinces, who were perceived to be docile and cheaper labor.

The situation was more sanguine for those who had climbed up to managerial or technical positions. However, elite women faced another kind of obstacle: they were not expected to be too "aggressive." Yu had worked as the workshop manager for years in the early 1980s and was about to be assigned as the new sales manager in the factory in 1985 when the previous manager took the leadership of

Table 3.1 Local and migrant wage workers in the sample in Bei Village

Born in	Gender	Number	1940s			1950s			1960s			1970s			1980s			1990s			2000s		
			P	L	M	P	L	M	P	L	M	P	L	M	P	L	M	P	L	M	P	L	M
1910s	M	3	33%	33%		67%	67%		33%	33%			33%			33%			33%			33%	
1910s	F	0	/	/		/	/		/	/		/	/		/	/		/	/		/	/	
1920s	M	6		17%			33%	17%		33%		17%	17%		17%	33%		/	/	/	/	/	/
1920s	F	2	/	/			50%	33%		33%			17%			33%			50%			50%	
1930s	M	15		13%		13%	27%	40%	20%	27%		33%	47%	20%	33%	27%		13%	13%	13%		20%	7%
1930s	F	6					17%			17%			17%			17%			17%			17%	
1940s	M	21	/	/	/		14%		14%	19%	10%	14%	29%	10%	24%	33%	19%	19%	24%	10%	14%	33%	10%
1940s	F	14	/	/		/	/			7%			21%			50%			57%			36%	
1950s	M	16	/	/	/	/	/	/	/	/	/	6%	50%	13%	13%	44%	31%	19%	50%	31%	6%	38%	18%
1950s	F	20	/	/		/	/		/	/			40%		5%	65%		5%	45%		5%	40%	
1960s	M	9	/	/	/	/	/	/	/	/	/	/	/	/		44%	22%	11%	11%	22%	22%	22%	
1960s	F	11	/	/		/	/		/	/		/	/			73%			56%			54%	
1970s	M	7	/	/	/	/	/	/	/	/	/	/	/	/	14%	14%	14%		29%	14%		43%	14%
1970s	F	8	/	/		/	/		/	/		/	/			13%			75%			25%	
Total		138																					

P = local managerial personnel, L = local wage worker, M = migrant worker.

Note: Among 85 couples, there were 77 men and 61 women (138 in total) who had complete working trajectory information. "/" means "not applicable," and the blank cells are used to refer to 0%.

the enterprise. But the village leader suggested that this position was not appropriate for a woman, and "even her husband would not agree," implicitly referring to the requirement to travel alone and be "active" outside. After failing to get this position, Yu worked very hard to climb up to another position, the production manager of the factory. Related to the small sizes of the local factories, there were not many managerial and professional positions for women to compete for, whereas the top leadership positions were mostly occupied by men. Although women were equally or even more active as local wage workers compared with men, they were underrepresented in the "managerial" positions, as shown in Table 3.1. Given the interaction of gender beliefs and the materialist orientation in the market economy, women were in general expected to generate stable and supplementary income.

The rise of private sectors

The nascent private sectors were rooted in the tradition of sidelines in peasant households. In the Maoist era, some villagers continued to multitask in private sidelines, mainly in an underground status and in self-employment forms. As the reform unfolded, the private sectors revived and expanded from those that relied more on individual work and family labor to those that hired other employees. They included enterprises that were transformed from the previously collective industries and those that were developed from individual or family ventures.

Table 3.2 shows that men and women had different patterns of being engaged in self-employment (mainly relied on the labor of the self and the family) and running private enterprises or businesses that hired some employees. In the pre-reform era, women had been more active in self-employment than men, and there had been no private entrepreneurs during that period, because "hiring employees" often involved political risks. Given the political environment, women took advantage of their flexibility to conduct self-employment activities that were informal, home-based, and extensions of family sidelines. But for men's craftsmanship and skills, they usually needed to rely on the collective patronage to work as temporary migrant workers or collective working teams rather than working on their own. The control on women was less tight, as their labor was related with lower work points and their flexible and multitasking working patterns were largely tolerated by the local state.

Starting in the 1980s, men became more active in both self-employment and running private enterprises, and in general, the gender gap was reversed at this time when women seemed to be less active in private sectors than men. This was because many women were absorbed into local factories and lost interest in doing "side jobs." Although factory jobs attracted many men as well, there was a stronger tendency among men to be their "own boss." Gen, a 59-year-old man when interviewed in 2004, had been determined to work for himself when he was young. He was introduced to work in a metal material factory in a nearby city in 1968 by a relative, and he paid one third of his salary to the production team to get the permission to work outside of the village. When the village began

Table 3.2 Self-employment and private business with hired employees in the sample in Bei Village

Born in	Gender	Number	1940s		1950s		1960s		1970s		1980s		1990s		2000s	
			S	E	S	E	S	E	S	E	S	E	S	E	S	E
1910s	M	3	/	/	/	/	/	/	/	/	/	/	/	/	/	/
	F	/	/	/	/	/	/	/	/	/	/	/	/	/	/	/
1920s	M	6			50%											
	F	2														
1930s	M	15	/	/	33%							7%	7%	7%	17%	
	F	6	/	/												
1940s	M	21	/	/	/	/	5%		14%		10%		14%	10%	14%	10%
	F	14	/	/	/	/	7%								36%	31%
1950s	M	16	/	/	/	/	5%		25%		6%		5%	5%	13%	5%
	F	20	/	/	/	/									10%	
1960s	M	9	/	/	/	/	/	/	/	/	11%	22%	11%	22%	22%	22%
	F	11	/	/	/	/	/	/	/	/	9%		9%	9%	22%	9%
1970s	M	7	/	/	/	/	/	/	/	/	/	/	14%	13%	29%	29%
	F	8	/	/	/	/	/	/	/	/	/	/			25%	
Total		138														

S = self-employed, E = private business with hired employees.

Note: Among 85 couples, there were 77 men and 61 women (138 in total) who had complete working trajectory information. "/" means "not applicable," and the blank cells are used to refer to 0%.

to establish collective enterprises, he was invited to return to the village to be a manager. Gen came back to work in a collective enterprise for several years, but soon quit to run his own workshop of construction materials, because he always desired the autonomy to run his own business. Many capable and skillful men who used to work in rural industries would quit and turn to their own businesses, unless they became the absolute boss in the previous enterprises they had worked for.

As private enterprises were increasingly legitimized and became the mainstream, the gender gap became more salient for private entrepreneurs than in self-employment. This was partly related to the male dominance in the leadership of previously collective industries. Through the process of privatization, previous male managers often took over the enterprises via the purchase of the enterprise. A few women entered the management team of the enterprise, but their positions were often to support male managers before the privatization, and then to support male entrepreneurs after the privatization. In addition to the previously collective enterprises, the newly rising private businesses were also mainly dominated by men. There were around 16 sizable private enterprises established by villagers in the 1990s and 2000s, and all of them were run by male entrepreneurs (Bei Village Archive Committee, 2007, pp. 139–140). This finding echoed previous studies that linked higher incomes with taking risks and stable jobs with passivity and femininity (Kim et al., 2010; Rofel, 1999).

However, a few women like Yu suggested that they had similar ambition to run their own businesses. These women were usually female cadres or factory managers and had access to some economic resources and organizational links. When they found it was difficult in wage sectors to have further career development or make a greater fortune, they might "jump into the sea (*xiahai*)" to start their own business. In 1990, Yu was already one of the managers in the electronic cord factory, and planned to quit her job and rent a salesroom for the textile trade. Although Yu described that she had been "satisfied as long as the wage was increasing over time," she wanted to have a change in her life. Eventually, Yu's employer persuaded her to stay in the factory with better rewards. But when interviewed in her fifties, Yu still regretted that she did not take the opportunity to leave the wage sector, "otherwise I would be a boss as well." Yu envied those who started their own businesses in the 1990s and achieved great market success afterward, and she felt that the 1990s was the "best" time to enter the market.

For women who "jumped into the sea," they were still more represented in self-employment than running bigger private businesses. At this time, traditional sidelines such as needlework had a more limited market and a narrower profit margin. Meanwhile, more capital-intensive types of self-employment emerged in the village, including trade and transportation. At the time around the 1990s, more villagers had accumulated economic resources and market experiences and were able to invest in more capital-intensive businesses, and they no longer needed to seek protection from collective patrons. But it was still not common for women to run big businesses and hire employees by themselves. There were only three women respondents who managed to lead private businesses that hired employees: one was a co-owner of the family trade business with her husband, one established a day care center with the help of her husband's networks, and the other was supported by her natal family's investment to run a clothes shop.

As such, family support was crucial for women to enter the increasingly capital-intensive private sectors. Yu did not "jump into the sea," partly because her husband did not want to support her in her market adventure. Yu married her husband in 1976 when he was a sent-down youth (*xiaxiang zhiqing*) from the nearby city. Although marrying a young man with urban connections was desir-able, Yu found that her husband was not good at catching economic opportuni-ties after the market was opened up. Yu's husband was satisfied with his wage job in a local economic cooperative which was gained through his urban connections, and he still believed that working in the urban "public" sectors (state-owned or collective work units) was more prestigious than rural industries and the private sector, which Yu had been working in and wanted to send their only daughter into.

Family battles ensued and were intensified when Yu's daughter entered the labor market in 1997. According to Yu, the father preferred work units "that would never go bankrupt," whereas Yu no longer believed in such an "iron rice bowl (*tiefanwan*)." She preferred a "rubber rice bowl" that allowed more elastic-ity for economic rewards in an era when higher income came with taking risks, and stability was an obstacle to success (Kim et al., 2010, p. 944). In fact, Yu became the family's major breadwinner and won support from her daughter. Despite her father's objections, Yu's daughter used Yu's connections to enter a rural textile factory and then began to run trade business for its sales depart-ment on a contract basis in 2001. She met her future husband in the factory, and the young couple made one million yuan of profit from their private business in 2004.

This case illustrates the interaction between gender norms and job hierarchies. Under the market reform, urban women generally preferred secure wage work rather than riskier jobs in the private sector (Kim et al., 2010, pp. 941–942). Market risk, as suggested by Zhang and Pan (2012), was a big concern for urban professional women, who were generally reluctant to leave their jobs. Rural women, however, commonly took greater responsibility for their own welfare and care arrangements, rather than counting on employers. As such, they were more ready to embrace opportunities in private sectors rather than stick to the wage sector, as did their urban counterparts. Yu intentionally transmitted her social capital in the wage sector to the private sector, and her daughter fulfilled her dream to "take big risks and make big money." As found in other studies, the children of entrepreneurs were brought into the transport and commercial sides of the business rather than into manufacturing (Bossen, 2002, p. 137). Although Yu did not become an entrepreneur by herself, her valuable experience, knowl-edge, and connections broadened the horizon of her daughter and facilitated her market adventure.

To deal with economic and ideological difficulties for women to start ventures, Yu's daughter benefited from economic and social resources that derived from her natal family; some other women joined family ventures based on the husband–wife collaboration. Wen (a 54-year-old woman when interviewed in 2005) is one of the women who dropped out of a factory and started a home business with her husband. She recalled:

> I worked in the factory for 10 years, until we started our business in 1994. . . . My husband used to be a migrant worker in the corrosion protection industry, and worked as a chef for a while. . . . Then we opened our own restaurant, beside the department of motor vehicles, and drivers would stop for meals frequently. It was very tiring but we made good income. . . . After two years we turned to other business, selling buns for breakfast in the town, and later taking over part of the school cafeteria on a lease.

In Wen's case, she gave up her own wage job to follow her husband, who used to be a chef and then wanted to open his own restaurant. Such cooperation was more common among older women, and they often regarded their labor as just "helping out" with more flexibility to accommodate family needs and typically accepted no personal remuneration. Wen was happy to run errands as long as they made a good income. These women's unpaid involvement in family ventures seemed to suggest that women's labor was again devalued and blended into multiple tasks, similar to the situation found in other studies that women accepted agricultural tasks as part of a housewife's work (Judd, 1990). But such "women's work" was not always invisible, and some male interviewees particularly expressed their gratitude to their hardworking wives, because "unlike men, women had heavier burdens, working all the time for the family."[14] Although it was rare for women to take the leading role in such family businesses, people often considered it just a division of labor that men dealt with external suppliers and clients and women were responsible for internal management.

Although usually not recognized as the nominal leaders, young women in bigger family ventures expected to have more control in the business compared with older women. These women still received no payment in general, but they tended to perceive their work to be of actual importance, such as overseeing the production or construction on the behalf of their husbands. For example, Suqin (a 42-year-old woman when interviewed in 2010) quit her factory job when she got married to a private contractor in 1992, and migrated to the city to cook for her husband's construction team. When she worked as a migrant worker in an urban factory, Suqin felt "rootless" and saw little chance of career development. Feeling like just a cog in a machine, Suqin was aware that she would eventually be abandoned when her labor was no longer needed. She was happy to cook for her husband's construction team, as she felt it meaningful to work for a place that she "belonged to." Suqin began to watch the construction site to avoid wasteful usage of construction materials, because "every small piece we save, it is in our pocket." However, when Suqin had her son in 1993, her mother-in-law refused to give up her factory job for unpaid grandparenting. Suqin had to wait until her son went to school to resume work. When she returned to the venture, she became better prepared. She learned how to drive workers to the construction site and brought her own brother into the business, which enabled her to exercise greater control over the family venture.

Given the prosperity of private business based on family cooperation, the ideal of honorable independent women was replaced by the appreciation of women who had responded more actively to family needs. As a new trend in the post-Mao era, many women turned their imaginations away from the supposedly glorious aspects of working outside the home and back to the domestic arena to renegotiate power with other family members (Wang, 2010, p. 970). Rather than directly challenging the "natural" gender division of labor, some women found niches of autonomy and authority within family businesses.

Adapting family strategies

Compared with other rural areas that mainly relied on exporting labor to urban centers, Bei Village provided ample local job opportunities. Meanwhile, the local industries were relatively small and provided limited room to climb up the career ladders, and many villagers had switched to the more flexible and profitable private sectors instead. These employment patterns were gendered, given women's activeness in local wage work, sidelines, and self-employment, and men's dominance in migrant work and bigger private businesses.

Despite the variety in the employment transition, changes in the family arena were relatively slow. In the Maoist era, the state "absorbed the most interior aspects of the private world in the political realm" following the socialist revolutions (Glosser, 2003, p. 174), but the traditional family roles for women and men remained to be important. As a result, women had to work double shifts in and outside home and were encouraged to overcome their biological obstacles. At the grassroots level, local offices had given discretion regarding women's labor participation to accommodate their family roles in different ways. Women's persisting "inside" roles created room to conduct income-generating activities in sideline, home-based, and self-employed forms in the pre-reform era. Although such economic activities were intentionally ignored by the local state, women's contributions were well recognized by family members.

In the market reform era, the traditions of patrilocal marriage and the inside-outside divide were redefined with a higher expectation of men's economic success. Men with market success became the most popular grooms in the marriage market, although the brides' economic contributions were also appreciated (Song & Luke, 2014). In the recent visits to the village, it was not rare to observe a husband in a private business of construction or corrosion protection to be paired with a wife in wage work, or a housewife who quit her previous job. Some women put on hold their own careers as factory workers, service clerks, or village doctors to be stay-at-home mothers when their husbands could make a fortune from private business.

Such a "traditional" division of labor reflected changes in both job hierarchies and family dynamics. First, private businesses were regarded highly and as more prestigious than other work, including white-collar wage work. This obscured and undermined the urban-rural boundary and the formal-informal job hierarchy deeply rooted in the Maoist era. Second, the dual-earner practice had been undermined by the tolerance of becoming a "housewife." Rural industrialization had made the dual-earner pattern popular in Bei Village in the 1980s, but the rise of private sectors also helped to strengthen the traditional expectation for women to retreat from the public sphere, with the new materialist orientation that valued the husband's success in private business.

Given stiffer competition over time, private sectors also became more capital-intensive. Unlike old women who could multitask in home-based sidelines to supplement the family incomes, young people either retreated from the business world or were attracted to it because they were more resourceful, dynamic, and less risk-averse. Young women who entered the private sector more recently tended to devote more time and energy to these ventures, rather than "helping out" in a supporting role, as the old generations of women described their participation in family ventures. Although often constrained by customary rights to access to productive capital (Bossen, 2002, p. 109), some women managed to oversee family economic and financial affairs. These women did not desire to challenge the position of the male family head who served as the public face of the business, but found room to exert their agency as the "family manager" (Cohen, 1992).

Although opportunities for women to accumulate substantial wealth in their own right remained limited given the patrilineal tradition of land and house inheritance (Bossen, 2002, p. 146), some women took advantage of family resources more flexibly given their close relations with their natal families. Haiping, a 36-year-old woman when interviewed in 2010, was supported by her natal family to establish her own clothes shop. Before that, she had spent a few years in a local factory and disliked to be "disciplined" in the workplace. In contrast, Haiping's parents and two elder sisters had been satisfied with their wage work and accumulated considerable wage savings. As the youngest daughter and the sweetheart of the family, Haiping got supported by her natal family because she was the only one who desired to run a shop. Haiping established her clothes shop at the age of 20, and similar to the case of Yu's daughter, family resources were passed on to daughters as there were no sons. The market success of these young women justified the families' decision to invest in their daughters' dreams, although such opportunities rarely existed for older generations of women.

The opportunities for young women were related to the fact that families had a declining number of children on average. The cohort of women in the sample who were born in the 1920s had around 4.6 children in their lifetime on average; for the cohort born in the 1940s, the average number of children was 2.7, whereas for the cohort born in the 1970s, the average number of children had decreased to 1 (Table 3.3). The value of daughters had been partly recognized before the market reform with their earning power in needlework, reinforced with rural industrialization. But when young women became mothers, they also

Table 3.3 Number of children in the sample in Bei Village

Mother born in	1		2		3		4		5 and more		Total	Average
1910s									100%		1	5
1920s							40%		60%		5	4.6
1930s					27%		36%		36%		11	3.7
1940s	5%		32%		53%		11%				19	2.7
1950s	25%		62%		13%						24	1.9
1960s	55%		45%								11	1.5
1970s	100%										8	1
Total	21	27%	26	33%	16	20%	8	10%	8	10%	79	

Note: The number of children is missing for 6 out of 85 couples, so there are 79 valid cases. If the mother's age is missing, the father's age is used as an approximate. The blank cells are used to refer to 0%.

tended to invest more into raising their precious children, and the importance of being a good mother could play a key role in women's self-fulfillment.

Not only did the family have fewer children but the family size also decreased over time in general. Given the family's growing financial capability in housing construction, many young couples split from the extended family in residence, even though they often ate together in the homes of parents or in-laws. Over time, the family size in the village had decreased from 5.5 persons in 1949, 4.3 persons in 1963, 4.1 persons in 1975, 3.5 persons in 1991, to 2.5 persons in 2006.[15] The decline of family size and the number of children had enabled some women to access more resources and gain more autonomy and decision-making power in the family.

These trends were manifested in the case of Haiping, who wanted to cultivate a comfortable family life by herself without the intervention of in-laws. When Haiping married a private contractor in 2000, she closed her shop because "the family life will be ruined if both spouses are work-obsessed, and I want to take care of my child, who is the only one. I should be in charge, not the grandma."[16] To Haiping, running a business and being a good mother were both her dreams of "being in charge." Although she put her own business on hold for the sake of her husband's business, she did not follow the ideal of the traditional homebound daughter-in-law. In line with Yan Yunxiang's arguments about "girl power" (Yan, 2006), young women experience the world in a way which makes them feel they have more freedom, but the new gender politics has been naturalized in a way that young women regard the investment in their precious children's needs as part of their own self-desires. Haiping's ability to move back and forth between these ambitions highlighted the quest for personal satisfaction among young women, which was denied by older women who spent their younger years "eating bitterness" (Wang, 2010, p. 962) under an ethic of hard work and self-sacrifice (Evans, 2010, p. 988).

By work intermittently, Haiping found a new way to balance family and work, and she planned to resume her business when her son reached school age. Unlike many rural women in other areas who needed to migrate for jobs, Haiping was confident that she could return to her business when she wanted to without worrying about the lack of economic opportunities. Compared with the prevalent multitasking strategy among old women, young women grew up in a deepening urban and consumerist culture with a focus on "individual goals and happiness" (Riley, 2012, p. 135). The move away from multitasking practices served their pursuit of more freedom, which meant that they refused to be tied to a workplace or to be subordinated to the in-laws.

But women's choice of working on-and-off also suggested that it was difficult to challenge the conventional division of labor between the husband and the wife. Even the ambitious and dynamic women who had achieved market success had been struggling to grapple with different gender and family ideologies. If the husband was a capable breadwinner like Wen's or Haiping's husband, many women would not object being the homemaker and putting their own careers on hold. Some women who wanted to continue working still had to rely on old women for the unpaid domestic work.

However, the different generations also began to pursue distinct and incompatible paths toward personal happiness (Wang, 2010, p. 961). As such, younger women's working patterns were mediated by the expectations and attitudes of their family members. Both Haiping and her husband favored Haiping's withdrawal from employment and longed for a cultivated family environment. Suqin was less willing to withdraw but she could not persuade her mother-in-law to give up her own earning opportunities for unpaid grandparenting. As such, women did not necessarily face an easier family–work balance over time. Compared with the older generation who were used to a double shift of work and family, the younger generation might be more active or passive in pursuing their own careers given the diverse forms of family division of labor contingent on values and behaviors of their family members.

Freedom, market risks, and safety nets

Bei Village had been a traditional grain-growing area with intensive labor investments. The family farm tenure was prolonged and stabilized in 1984 given the central government policy, and many respondents mentioned that they desired the "freedom" to operate outside of the collective economy and move away from farming. Given the traditions of sidelines and craftsmanship, villagers valued working on their own rather than as part of the collective in trying out different market opportunities. As a result, many peasants had given away part of their land, and such informal arrangements were complemented by the village coordination in taking back and leasing land on a contract basis to individual managerial farmers.

Greater freedom to move away from farming was achieved when most of the village's land was included in the suburban greenbelt zone in 2003. But different from land expropriation elsewhere, the rezoning occurred based on a 20-year contract between the district government and the village council. In other words, land remained collectively owned and the village could continue to reap benefits in the future with the renewal of the land contract and the increase in land prices.

Despite the relatively egalitarian compensation derived from land transfer, the village had witnessed rapid stratification, especially between the "private bosses" and those who "earned wages." Along with the privatization of rural industries and the influx of migrant workers from the poor inland areas, many villagers lost interest in wage jobs in rural industries and turned to private business, and factories began to recruit more migrant workers from the outside. When asked why someone could be the "boss" whereas others were not, respondents tended to attribute it to their courage, resources, and good timing to make investments. As Yu suggested, those who could "make big money" were those who dare to take "big risks." This partly explained why villagers felt that women were not suitable to run private businesses. This was to some extent a replication of the urban division of women's stable work and men's risky work, but rural women were more ready to embrace challenging jobs in the private sectors due to the limited welfare from rural employers (Song, 2015). Some women did have the desire to be their own boss. Some were the old economic elites like Yu, who had been a Maoist activist and a representative of women's home-based needlework and felt frustrated about the glass ceiling in her managerial work in a factory. Some others were young dynamic women like Haiping, who hated to be a factory worker and had sufficient resources from her natal family. As such, women could draw on different resources and values to support themselves to be courageous and daring to take market risks. Still, women's economic power often got "discounted" by larger social forces and norms of the existing gender stratification (Blumberg, 1991; Coleman, 1991; Riley, 2012, p. 86).

As running private business was considered more promising than climbing career ladders in wage sectors, people had often valued direct market experiences over education. It was illustrated by the comparison between the highest education levels within the couples in the sample (the higher education level of the spouses, either the husband or the wife) and that of their children (the highest level among the children). Thirty-seven percent of couples had only primary school education, 28 percent had middle school education, 6 percent had high school education, and only 3 percent went to universities. Some factory workers in rural industries taught themselves to operate and fix machines when they were required to become technicians. For those who ran their own businesses, they valued skills and connections developed from real market experiences. But in general, these villagers wanted to prepare their children better to deal with the stiffer market competition, and they were able to invest more in their children with their increased wealth. Among respondents, 16 percent of the families sent their children to high schools and 25 percent to universities, in addition to those who were still in schools, which represents 26 percent of the families. As the rural economy and private sectors were increasingly legitimated and institutionalized, villagers hoped that their children could occupy a better position not only in terms of incomes but also with higher social prestige. The intergenerational transmission of resources was also directed to daughters as well as sons. With Yu's social connections, Yu's daughter was introduced into a big rural factory after she graduated from a vocational college, where she could have a higher starting point by working for the sales department. In Yu's generation, rural families had sent the most capable laborers to muddle through the market against the institutional barriers and market uncertainties, and they wanted to help their children to sail through the market with new opportunities, although young people faced new challenges and increasing inequalities.

Given the increasing stratification among villagers, the village was to some extent atomized. Not only ordinary villagers but also village cadres suggested that they were more interested in their own individual and family interests rather than collective affairs. Such "selfish" tendencies used to be criticized by the Maoist ethics of self-sacrifice and devotion to collective goals, but were increasingly justified by the prevailing discourse of "market efficiency" and the privatization processes. To deal with the market uncertainties in an increasingly privatized economy, the village still needed to add to the basic safety net particularly for old and low-income villagers. Starting in 2001, the village council issued the "village pension," a monthly subsidy of 100 yuan, to the elderly (men aged above 60 and women aged above 55), which was increased to 200 yuan in 2005. In addition to that, ordinary villagers had enjoyed a yearly subsidy of 150 yuan from the collective since 2003.

Taking the local income level into consideration, the amount of subsidies was small, but villagers were relatively satisfied with their village welfare. These villagers were used to relying on themselves and their families for economic security. Furthermore, the village safety nets were added by the new rural cooperative medical insurance system and new rural pension insurance system promoted by local governments. Along with the land development around 2003, villagers were included in the elderly pension insurance system for the local "landless" peasants, in addition to receiving the yearly land compensation. Since 2005, most villagers were enrolled in the new cooperative medical insurance system as promoted by the city government.

The family and community strategies to deal with market risks could be traced back to the unique industrialization and privatization processes in Bei Village. Such development patterns allowed women's flexible labor that was compatible with their family roles. In the Maoist era, women's flexibility had been their advantage to sidestep institutional barriers and take a lead in developing home-based sidelines. The rise of rural industries allowed women to become local wage workers along with their male counterparts, but also continued the multitasking practices particularly for women. With the privatization of rural industries and the rise of the capital-intensive private sectors in the 1990s, men were perceived to be more suitable to take the leadership in risky and rewarding ventures. Younger women tended to work on-and-off, balancing their career pursuits and their desire to be good mothers. Although some resourceful and dynamic women were attracted to private businesses based on individual and family accumulations, frequently observed among women were career disruptions due to childbearing, childrearing, and grandparenting. At the family level, the loss in their earnings could be made up by the less interrupted careers of other family members, which might reinforce the husband's role as the breadwinner and the family's role as the final provider of economic security. Although women had been creative and innovative in their economic activities, their economic power was discounted by family expectations and social norms such as the distaste for "aggressive women."

But some women also began to emphasize the sense of individualistic achievement as found in other studies (Hansen & Pang, 2010; Rofel, 1997). Given the individualization of the "modern" work (Riley, 2012, p. 100) and the decline of family sizes, these women might have received better education and more investment from their natal families to pursue their own careers. Other women got access to new economic opportunities in family businesses without directly challenging conventional gender norms. In the related husband-wife partnership, women might soften their approach to business by aiming at improving the family's welfare and meeting its needs. As such, family goals and individual goals could be mixed to defend women's choices, either to pursue market success or to work intermittently. For both men and women, the Maoist work ethic of devotion to the public sphere had given way to a tendency to avoid "wasting time" in public affairs for practical reasons, and had been overridden by individual and family calculations of material rewards.

Notes

1 The city has three districts, two county-level cities and one county.
2 Bei Village Archive Committee. 2007. *Bei Village Archive*. Beijing: Yanjiu Press, p. 60.
3 Ibid., p. 163.
4 Shaoxing Bureau of Statistics (Shaoxing shi tongjiju). 2006. *Shaoxing Economic and Social Development Statistics Report 2006 (Shaoxing shi 2006nian guominjingji he shehuifazhan tongji gongbao)*. Retrieved August 15, 2016 from www.tjcn.org/tjgb/11zj/1382.html
5 Zhejiang Bureau of Statistics (Zhejiang sheng tongjiju). 2006. *Zhengjiang Economic and Social Development Statistics Report 2006 (2006nian zhejiangsheng guominjingji he shehuifazhan tongji gongbao)*. Retrieved September 29, 2016 from www.zj.stats.gov.cn/tjgb/gmjjshfzgb/200703/t20070313_122156.html
6 Bei Village Archive, pp. 98–99. 1 mu = 0.16 acre or 666.7 square meters."
7 The local archive "Historical Scratch of Agricultural Output in Bei Village."
8 Interview with Yaotang, 2009; Aifeng, 2005; Baolin, 2005; Jinlin, 2009.
9 The work point system was conducted under the collective farming system to estimate the contributions from everyone participating in collective farming. Usually the work point system used a typical day of work by a full-time laborer as the standard for calculation (10 points), and one could earn 0–10 points depending on one's labor performance. Later on, the collective rewarded its members (food supplies and cash) based on the sum of work points one earned.
10 Bei Village Archive, p. 147.
11 Ibid., p. 102.
12 Ibid.
13 Women's tasks often faded into the background of house and courtyard work (Bossen, 2002, p. 104).
14 Interview with Guanlin, 2005.
15 Bei Village Archive, p. 60.
16 Interview with Haiping, 2010.

References

Bei Village Archive Committee (2007). *Bei Village Archive*. Beijing: Yanjiu Publisher.

Blumberg, R. L. (1991). Income under female versus male control: Hypotheses from a theory of gender stratification and data from the third world. In R. L. Blumberg (Ed.), *Gender, family, and economy: The triple overlap* (pp. 97–127). Newbury Park, CA: Sage.

Bossen, L. (2002). *Chinese women and rural development*. Lanham, MD: Rowman and Littlefield.

Cohen, M. (1992). Family management and family division in contemporary rural China. *The China Quarterly, 130*, 357–377.

Coleman, M. (1991). Division of household labor: Suggestions for future empirical consideration and theoretical development. In R. L. Blumberg (Ed.), *Gender, family, and economy: The triple overlap* (pp. 245–260). Newbury Park, CA: Sage.

Evans, H. (2010). The gender of communication: Changing expectations of mothers and daughters in urban China. *The China Quarterly, 204*, 980–1000.

Glosser, S. L. (2003). *Chinese visions of family and state, 1915–1953* (Vol. 5). Berkeley: University of California Press.

Hansen, M. H., & Pang, C. (2010). Idealizing individual choice: Work, love, and family in the eyes of young, rural Chinese. In M. H. Hansen & R. Svarverud (Eds.), *iChina: The rise of the individual in modern Chinese society* (pp. 39–64). Copenhagen: NIAS Press.

Judd, E. R. (1990). Alternative development strategies for women in rural China. *Development and Change, 21*(1), 23–42.

Kim, S. W., Vanessa, L. F., Hirokazu, Y., Niobe, W., Chen, X. Y., Deng, H. H., & Lu, Z. H. (2010). Income, work preferences and gender roles among parents of infants in urban China: A mixed method study from Nanjing. *The China Quarterly, 204*, 939–959.

Lardy, N. R. (1985). State intervention and peasant opportunities. In W. L. Parish (Ed.), *Chinese rural development* (pp. 33–56). Armonk, NY: M.E. Sharpe.

Li, H., & Rozelle, S. (2003). Privatizing rural China: Insider privatization, innovative contracts and the performance of township enterprises. *The China Quarterly, 176*, 981–1005.

Li, Y. (1994). "Nvren huijia" wenti zhiwojian (My views about "women returning home"). *Sociological Research, 6*, 71–72.

Oi, J. C. (1992). Fiscal reform and the economic foundations of local state corporatism in China. *World Politics, 45*(1), 99–126.

Riley, N. E. (2012). *Gender, work, and family in a Chinese economic zone: Laboring in paradise*. Wiesbaden: Springer Science & Business Media.

Rofel, L. (1997). Rethinking modernity: Space and factory discipline in China. In A. Gupta & J. Ferguson (Eds.), *Culture, power, place: Explorations in critical anthropology* (pp. 155–178). Durham, NC: Duke University Press.

Rofel, L. (1999). *Other modernities: Gendered yearnings in China after socialism*. Berkeley: University of California Press.

Song, J. (2015). Women and self-employment in post-socialist rural China: Side job, individual career or family venture. *The China Quarterly, 221*, 229–242.

Song, J., & Luke, N. (2014). Fairy brides from heaven: Mate selection in rural China, 1949–2000. *Journal of Comparative Family Studies, XLV*(4), 497–515.

Wang, D. N. (2010). Intergenerational transmission of family property and family management in urban China. *The China Quarterly, 204,* 960–979.

Yan, Y. (2006). Girl power: Young women and the waning of patriarchy in rural north China. *Ethnology, 45*(2), 105–123.

Zhang, Q. F., & Pan, Z. (2012). Women's entry into self-employment in urban China: The role of family in creating gendered mobility patterns. *World Development, 40*(6), 1201–1212.

4 Su Village

Collective legacy and the "new socialist countryside"

Su Village is located in the southeast of Jiangsu Province. It is in the northeast of the city of Suzhou, an area famous for fertile soil and delicate textiles. The village is 61 kilometers away from Suzhou and 15 kilometers from the county seat of Grain City (a county-level city). In the series of development zoning and rezoning processes, the rural townships in the locality had been transformed into big towns, and people in these suburban towns were allowed to buy an urban household registration status. By 2003, within a local population of 24,000 people in White Town (where Su Village is located), around half of them had an urban hukou. The town also accommodated 17,000 migrant workers from other places to work in the local industries. These industries were gradually moved to the town's industrial zone, which occupied one fourth of the town's land (10,000 mu out of 40,000 mu).[1] In 2003, White Town was merged into Old Town. Within the new big town, the rezoning practice continued: small villages were merged into big villages, and then 3 of the villages were rezoned into semi-urban communities under the governance of the town.

In Su Village, most residents continue to hold their rural hukou, but the urban-rural gap has been greatly reduced due to rural industrialization. The village has around 410 households, 13 villagers' groups (or teams), and 1,700 people.[2] The annual income per capita of Su Village had reached around 10,000 yuan in 2006, higher than the average income of around 9,300 yuan in Grain City[3] and the provincial average of 5,813 yuan.[4] Under the official agenda of constructing the "new socialist countryside," Su Village had redirected its industrial revenues toward organizing the scaling-up of agriculture and conducting "modern" housing projects, which made the village membership more beneficial over time.

The field visits were carried out in 2003, 2004, 2005, 2006, and 2010. The interviews were collected with 46 families: for 34 of them, the husband was the main respondent; in 11 families, the wife was the main respondent; in 1 family, both the husband and the son were interviewed. In total, there were 36 men and 11 women among the respondents (47 persons in total). The age of the wife ranged from 28 to 69 at the time of the investigation, and the age of the husband ranged from 24 to 77. Among the respondents, 5 were villager cadres and local officials who provided more information on local economic structures and development pathways.

Collective farms, household farms, and managerial farms

The Suzhou area has been the most well-developed farming area, which had "fed" the country and been subject to heavy agricultural extraction since the Song Dynasty (around the 1200s). Its favorable growing conditions, including fertile soil and plentiful water supply, were closely related to its traditional two-season grain production. Following the socialist transformation in the countryside, governments relied on areas like Su Village heavily for grain production to feed the nation and fuel urban industrialization. The local state exerted various measures to mobilize peasants into collective agriculture, and little space was left for underground sideline activities.

The collective farms were redistributed to households from 1982 to 1983,[5] and peasants were soon exempted from paying agricultural taxes because the village leadership was able to redirect its industrial revenues to pay on the behalf of peasant households until it was removed around 2005. Despite such favorable moves to promote peasants' incentives to farm, industrialization inevitably distracted local people from their farming responsibility. As farming required patience to wait for limited income after year-round cultivation and harvesting, and its profits were often constrained by low prices of agricultural products, the households would send the most capable workers to the new industrial sectors (as found in other studies, see Murphy, 2002). Farming responsibility also declined with land development to construct factories and roads along with industrialization, and the amount of farming land had decreased from 3300 mu in 1999, to 2700 mu in 2003, and 2200 mu in 2012.[6] At the time of the interview, respondents reported that the land per capita varied from 1 to 1.5 mu,[7] depending on changes in family structures after land redistribution.

The development-oriented campaigns, however, were adjusted from time to time for other policy concerns such as food security. In Su Village, land expropriation for industrial or commercial use had been occasionally carried out since the 1990s but with increasing caution, and the cost of land expropriation increased dramatically. To curb the loss of agricultural land, the central government had moved toward more stringent land expropriation policies. In particular, the government set up "red line zones" (*hongxianqu*) of agricultural land, which meant land that could not be "touched," and the policy was formalized in 2006. In 2013, of the land in Jiangsu province, 22.2 percent was confirmed to belong to "red line zones."[8]

Given the coexisting policy priorities of encouraging economic development and reserving agricultural land, the village leadership adapted their land use practices in a flexible way to make the full use of economic resources and to free surplus laborers, such as by allowing the transfer of land between peasant households. Despite the general labor flows out of the agricultural sector and the desire to leave the farming tasks behind, some peasants wanted to grow more land, and the "land-missing" and "land-cherishing" mood was not uncommon among the old generations. The land transfer between households used to be informal based on private negotiations, and some managerial farmers took over small pieces of family farms with little payments.

Since 2004, such practices began to be coordinated by the village office, and the village leadership turned to a more centralized "land transfer" system and signed contracts with the managerial farmers, once every three or five years.[9] To compensate the households who gave up their use rights of the land, the "transfer fee" (*liuzhuanfei*) increased from 150 yuan to 300 yuan per mu every year, first applied in a 500-mu project to grow asparagus. The land transfer price was increased to 420 yuan per mu in 2005, largely due to the increase of grain prices in 2004. The change in grain prices also resulted in the increasing interests among peasants in farming, and they requested to become managerial farmers themselves. In 2005, the village leadership had to redistribute the land to villagers who wanted to be managerial farmers, and limited the scale of managerial farming (adjusted from a range of 50–80 mu to 30–50 mu) and the length of the contract period (three years).[10] As a result, the village leadership rented around 1,000 mu of the land to about 20 managerial farmers.[11]

In this process, land transfer was not only institutionalized and practiced on large scales, but also supported with government subsidies to promote managerial farming. In 2005, the land transfer price was increased to 450 yuan per mu, of which managerial farmers paid 150 yuan, and the remaining 300 yuan was covered by government subsidies. In 2009, the transfer fee was increased to 600 yuan per mu by the city government and half was paid by government subsidies, according to the village accountant.[12] If their farms were of larger scales, they would benefit from more favorable policies and subsidies from governments. In recent years, the profitability of farming declined again. In Su Village, the amount of farming land had been stabilized at around 2,200 mu. By 2010, most of the land in the village had been taken by managerial farmers, but with the monopoly of the biggest agricultural corporation. This agricultural corporation was supported by local governments to promote "organic agriculture" in several villages, including Su Village, and the agricultural corporation had worked closely with the village office in negotiating compensation and defining contract length.

To some extent, the scaling-up of agriculture was part of the "administrative performance" of the local state, and it led to different responses among men and women of different generations. Meiya was a 31-year-old woman when interviewed in 2010, working as an accountant in the local clothes corporation, and her parents kept moving back and forth between farm work and factory jobs. The family used to have 5 mu of family farm in the 1980s, with a division of Meiya's mother in farm work and domestic work and her father in factory work. When Meiya's mother became a factory worker as well in the 1990s, the family "gave away" part of their farm to their neighbors. But in 1996, the couple saw a chance of managerial farming and moved to another town to rent 20 mu of land. During the same time, they sent their only daughter, Meiya, to a vocational school, where she received education in accounting and became an accountant in the clothes corporation in 1999. In 2001, Meiya's father also joined the enterprise as a salesperson, while her mother continued to take care of the managerial farms, but relying more on the mechanized farming system and the employed laborers.

In Meiya's case, her father moved to factory work, then to managerial farming, and then to a wage job again, but her mother was either left-behind or following the husband when the new opportunities seemed more promising. It was common that women used to be the ones who "filled in" the positions as required by the family economy, but Meiya did not want to be as "fully occupied" with the tedious and boring working cycles as her mother did outside and inside the home. Young people typically chose to work full-time outside the home rather than multitasking in farming regardless of their gender, which was often the hope of their parents as well.

Collective patronage, managers, and entrepreneurs

The village collective had played an important role not only in coordinating land distribution but also in industrialization. Before the market reform, only a few tailors, carpenters, and barbers were allowed to move and sell their services under the permission of the production teams, and they handed in part of their income to the production teams in exchange for the "work points" that would be converted into food supplies. Later on, these villagers were organized into a "craftsmen's" team under the brigade (the agricultural production unit at the village level under the collective farming system) in 1972, which was transformed into collective workshops later as part of the collective economy. The major part of the collective economy, however, had been the textile factories in the early reform years.

The village leader at that time, Meijing, a 69-year-old woman when interviewed in 2004, was one of the female political stars in the locality under the Maoist ideology of "women holding up half the sky." Seeing the village suffering from poverty and bounded in farming, Meijing had courageously gathered information about urban factories in the 1970s in order to find a market niche. In 1974, the village leadership secretly traded its tractor for a textile machine with an urban factory, and started the first cotton mill workshop. Given the political risks of developing rural industries, such workshops had been operated under the collective patronage, and the village leadership identified some "capable" activists and assigned them to be collective managers.

Gubo, a 60-year-old man when interviewed in 2005, was the first collective manager of the cotton mill. He benefited from the Maoist education program to favor "the offspring of poor peasants" in education and spent two and a half years in middle school, then dropped out in 1961 at the age of 16. As an active young man with some decent education, he became the secretary of the youth league in the village and was considered the ideal candidate for managing the workshop. His basic knowledge of machine operation and networking skills with urban technicians and clients proved to be of great help in turning the factory into a big success in the 1980s. Afterwards, Gubo established several other textile factories within the collective economy, among which a knitwear factory was later most successful and remained under his management.

The close connection between cadres and managers in the collective economy contributed to a unique pattern of industrialization process in Su Village. Such a pattern was commonly reported in the southern Jiangsu area and was summarized as the *Sunan model*, in which the collective legacy played a key role in the rapid growth of rural industries (Fei, 1983). Such developmental patterns were echoed by "local state corporatism" (Oi, 1992), i.e., the local state was a unit maximizing its interests differently from the central state. However, the local state was not a unitary and stable decision-making unit but included multiple actors within the collective economy, and the interaction between managers and cadres within local state corporatism, and their relationships with higher authorities, underwent fundamental changes over time.

The more recent developments in rural industries reflected the changing relationships among the village office, managers, and higher authorities. Over time, managers wanted to have more autonomy from the collective economy, and there was less overlapping between economic and political elites. The market success of the former continued to be used to prove the administrative performance of the latter, but the enterprises no longer needed the protection of the village collective to survive and develop. Due to the changing power relations, the higher authorities wanted to mobilize and utilize the resources and networks owned by the enterprises to serve the government goals of economic development and social stability, and began to co-optate these economic elites as the "political stars" to supplement or replace the previous leaders in the local office.

Gubo was absorbed into the village office as the vice party secretary and then the party secretary in 1990. But over time, the economic performance of the textile factories established by Gubo gradually gave way to the success of another factory, the clothes factory. The entrepreneur in the clothes factory became another political star, and he was elected to be the village party secretary in 1998. The succession of the village leadership was in line with the logic of market efficiency, and it served the government goals to co-optate the most successful entrepreneurs.

The reinforcement of the connection between entrepreneurs and the community played an important role in the era of the privatized rural economy. The village leadership had established around 12 enterprises throughout the 1970s and 1980s, and after the failure of some enterprises, there remained to be 3 big enterprises and 7 small enterprises, and all of them were privatized in the 1990s. The clothes factory was transformed into a big corporation group including two factories (still the two largest enterprises in the village), and the third big enterprise was the knitwear factory established by Gubo. The privatization was followed by an increase in private entrepreneurs, many of whom were transformed from collective managers (Table 4.1). Although the rural collective economic system in Jiangsu was maintained longer than most other areas of China (Su, 2009), its foundation had adapted from relying on the integrated cadre-manager leadership system to a more market-oriented co-optation system.

The co-optation of top entrepreneurs was important for the collective well-being of the village. Compared with small enterprises which needed to pay rents for the village's land and factory workshops, which added up to around 0.5 million yuan in 2005,[13] the clothes corporation was able to contribute 20 million

Table 4.1 Local entrepreneurs and managerial positions in the sample in Su Village

Born in	Gender	Number	1950s		1960s		1970s		1980s		1990–1997		1998–2010	
			E	M	E	M	E	M	E	M	E	M	E	M
1920s	M	1		100%		100%		100%		100%				
	F	2	50%	50%	50%	50%	50%	50%	50%	50%		50%		50%
1930s	M	2	50%	50%	50%	50%	50%	50%	50%	50%		50%		50%
	F	1		100%		100%		100%		100%		100%		
1940s	M	12			17%	33%	8%	58%	8%	67%	17%	83%	17%	67%
	F	8			13%	13%		13%		13%		13%	13%	13%
1950s	M	10	/	/			10%	30%	10%	30%	20%	30%	40%	40%
	F	6	/	/							33%		17%	17%
1960s	M	6	/	/	/	/						67%	17%	67%
	F	2	/	/	/	/								50%
1970s	M	8	/	/	/	/	/	/			25%		63%	38%
	F	7	/	/	/	/	/	/			14%	14%	14%	29%
1980s	M	6	/	/	/	/	/	/	/	/			33%	17%
	F	5	/	/	/	/	/	/	/	/				
Total		76												

E = local entrepreneurs and private businesspersons, M = local managerial positions.

Note: Among 46 couples, there were 45 men and 31 women (76 in total) who had complete working trajectory information. The final period started from 1998 because that was the year when the privatization was mostly completed. "/" means "not applicable," and the blank cells are used to refer to 0%.

yuan to the collective budget to finance the collective housing project in 1999.[14] The big enterprises were also the biggest local employers not only for the village but also for the locality, which was related to the greater support these enterprises got from local governments.

In spite of rising entrepreneurship, women rarely acted as the leading figures. In the Maoist era, some women had played key roles as cadres in developing nascent industries (see Table 4.1 for women born in the 1920s and 1930s in the sample). But with the development of collective enterprises, the management and operation of factories were mostly men's jobs, and men were often considered the suitable persons to operate and fix machines, which were the most precious resources in nascent industries. In the processes of privatization, most collective enterprises were taken over by male managers. After privatization, the gender gap in the number of entrepreneurs became more salient among respondents. For those born in the 1950s in the sample, the percentage of entrepreneurs and businesspersons was 40 percent for men and 17 percent for women after 1998 (compared with 20 percent for men and 33 percent for women before 1998). In this cohort, two more men became entrepreneurs in the privatization process, but one woman who used to run a store quit to join the clothes corporation for a stable wage job. For those born in the 1970s, the proportion of entrepreneurs and businesspersons was 63 percent for men and 14 percent for women after 1998 (compared with 25 percent for men and 14 percent for women before 1998). The number of male entrepreneurs and businesspersons increased from two to five (out of eight in this cohort), while there continued to be one woman entrepreneur (out of seven in this cohort). The gender gap in managerial positions, however, was smaller in some cohorts (67 percent for men and 50 percent for women among those born in the 1960s, and 38 percent for men and 29 percent for women among those born in the 1970s, but 17 percent for men and 0 percent for women among those born in the 1980s). The gender gap in managerial positions will be discussed in the following discussion of wage work.

Meanwhile, there were limited efforts by both men and women to start new ventures. The careers of small businesses owners were often perceived to be less attractive than the "good" jobs in big factories, which were stable and prestigious and had good income. Some respondents who were running small enterprises often complained about market risks, and sometimes thought about whether they should quit their ventures to try alternative jobs.[15] Since the privatization, the number of small enterprises increased only from 7 to 10 in the recent decades. The number of big enterprises has been stable since then, and villagers desired to take managerial and white-collar positions within them. Such jobs were rarely available to peasants in other rural areas in China, and were highly regarded by villagers.

Wage work and white-collar jobs in rural industries

In the nascent rural industries, job allocation had been a collective-dominated process. Those with a close connection with the village leadership, such as party members and activists, were likely to be privileged to become the first wage work-ers,[16] but such opportunities soon expanded to ordinary villagers. When villagers reached the working age, it was quite easy for them to get a wage job in local factories. Such an expectation remained after privatization, but wage work was no longer obtained via collective allocation but through the factories' regular recruitment processes. In this process, the village membership could still largely guarantee the entry into the factory, but was less influential in the subsequent promotion processes. At the factory floor level, enterprises began to recruit migrant workers from inland areas to supplement local workers, particularly in the big enterprises that witnessed great expansion in the 1990s and 2000s. For example, the clothes corporation employed around 8,000 workers at the time of this investigation, including around 6,000 workers who migrated from outside of the local county-level city.[17]

There were few complaints from villagers that their jobs were being taken over by migrant workers, as the villagers were less interested in the factory floor jobs. In fact, many villagers had climbed up to managerial or white-collar jobs in these enterprises. Some of them benefited from their local connections and early entries into the enterprises, and climbed up the job ladders based on their long-time service and their related experiences and networks. But for the new recruits, edu-cation was more important. Along with the expansion and institutionalization of the management systems, the managerial and professional positions in the clothes corporation had been dominated by university graduates.[18] These managerial and professional staff included some migrants who were recruited from the outside, but most staff remained locals.

Compared with other rural areas, local people had relatively modest to high education levels, as many parents were willing to and could afford to invest in their children's education. For the highest education level for the two spouses in the sample of 46 couples,[19] 20 percent of them had primary school educa-tion, 51 percent had middle school education, 17 percent had high school education, and 7 percent had a university degree or above. For the highest education level for the next generation in these families,[20] 5 percent had high school education, 27 percent went to universities, and the percentage would continue to increase because in 55 percent of the families, their children were still attending schools at the time of the investigation. The ample opportunities of getting a local wage job also relieved the anxiety to earn immediate income and allowed young people to extend their education to be more prepared for the local market.

Many local youth with a university or vocational school degree became clerks or salespersons in the big enterprises and thus avoided floor-level jobs. Several female white-collar workers in the clothes corporation indicated that, as local villagers, it was easy to enter local enterprises. But at the same time, they were also clearly aware that to get a better job, they had to attain certain education qualifications, and some of them had planned for this since they were in middle school. The locals' insider benefits and their investment in education combined to shape a new stratification pattern in which local people had a greater chance of job mobility, while migrant workers from other areas tended to take over those jobs in the lower tier of the labor market.

Compared with locals who occupied the managerial or white-collar positions based on their early entries or their education, ordinary local workers also benefited from their village membership: they were not easily fired when they got old, which was another practice that helped to defend the interests of "insiders." For example, the knitwear factory had around 300 workers, 75 percent of whom were still local villagers, and 25 percent migrant workers.[21] Some local workers had worked in the factories for decades, and they could still handle some simple or repetitive tasks in the factory, such as packaging. The knitwear factory reserved such positions for the old local workers by providing a less competitive level of wage.

Through being protective or disciplinary in different ways, these factory regimes had differentiated their employees by their place of origin, age, gender, and education, all affecting their perceived capabilities and merits. For local people, stable wage work was easily available and they would not be easily fired when they aged. For women in the sample who were born in the 1950s, the proportion who had a local job remained 33 percent in their 20s, 30s, and 40s, and increased to 50 percent in their 50s. For those who were born in the 1960s, the local wage job holders counted for 50 percent in their 20s, 30s, and 40s (Table 4.2). Men's representation in local wage work was less stable and even declined when they aged. This was partly related with the huge demand of women workers in the front-line jobs in the textile workshops, while men mostly worked as technicians, transporters, and security guards, who were smaller in numbers. It was also partly related with the significant increase in men's representation in managerial and entrepreneurial positions (Table 4.1).

With the expansion of local enterprises and the complication of career ladders, a new gender division had emerged. Among the managerial and white-collar positions, salespersons and managers who were sent to other areas were mostly men, and women were more likely to be in positions of locally based managers and clerks. Such a division of labor existed in several young couples in the sample in which the wife was interviewed while the husband was away at factory bases or trade centers in other cities. Meiya and her husband were one of such "long-distance" couples.

Meiya and her husband had worked in two departments in the clothes corporation. They got married in 2001 after Meiya had worked there for two years. In 2002, Meiya's husband was sent to the city of Changchun as a sales manager, and he had worked there for eight years until the time of this investigation. Meiya's husband usually spent several weeks every three months at home to take care of local management tasks. Related with this high mobility, Meiya's husband had a higher income than locally based managers or clerks like Meiya, and depending on the sales outcome, Meiya's husband enjoyed a big potential of bonus. Meiya indicated that it was widely accepted that men were more suitable to take up the roles of managers or salespersons to be sent to other cities and needed to travel a lot, travel alone, build connections in another city, recruit workers, and find new clients and partners. Despite her husband's earning capability, Meiya did

Table 4.2 Local and migrant wage workers in the sample in Su Village

Born in	Gender	Number	<20 (the age of respondents)		20s		30s		40s		50s		60s and above	
			Local	Migrant	Local	Migrant	Local	Migrant	Local	Migrant	Local	Migrant	Local	Migrant
1920s	M	1												
	F	2												
1930s	M	2			50%		50%						50%	
	F	1												
1940s	M	12	8%		33%	8%	25%		25%		8%		63%	
	F	8						13%[1]		13%[1]		13%[1]		13%[1]
1950s	M	10	10%		20%	10%	40%		40%		10%		/	/
	F	6			33%		33%		33%		50%		/	/
1960s	M	6	33%	33%	33%	17%	50%		50%		/	/	/	/
	F	2			50%						/	/	/	/
1970s	M	8	13%		50%				/	/	/	/	/	/
	F	7	29%	14%[2]	14%	14%[2]	43%	14%[2]	/	/	/	/	/	/
1980s	M	6	17%		67%	17%	/	/	/	/	/	/	/	/
	F	5	20%		80%		/	/	/	/	/	/	/	/
Total		76												

Notes: Among 46 couples, there were 45 men and 31 women (76 in total) who had complete working trajectory information. "/" means "not applicable," and the blank cells are used to refer to 0%.

[1] This percent indicates an exceptional case of one woman who worked outside the village: she was a sent-down youth and got an urban job due to policies to take care of sent-down youth.

[2] This percent indicates an exceptional case of one woman who worked outside the village: she used to work in a local optical cable factory and was sent to a branch office elsewhere.

not want to follow her husband as a housewife. She would rather stay in a long-distance relationship, because she had her own career, which was based locally.

The prevalence of formal jobs outside home enabled men and women to pursue their seemingly independent careers rather than working on family-based ventures. Women employees earned a separate amount of income independent from their husbands', and their contributions to the family were more visible. Old women who were less competitive in the labor market remained active in some wage jobs that were either part-time or physically less demanding, reserved for them in local industries. Compared with older cohorts, more young women had moved toward higher tiers in the factory regime, in a pattern similar to their male counterparts. However, the gender gap was still manifested by different "roles" they took up in the managerial positions.

In addition to the typical pathway of finding a local wage job, some young men, particularly those born in the 1970s and the 1980s, expressed a desire to try other opportunities in big cities, such as seeking employment in governments, state enterprises, or foreign companies, and a few of them had also planned to run small businesses. Meanwhile, they were aware that whenever they failed in the external labor market, they could always return to the village and get factory work, and this fallback option was largely guaranteed by their village membership. Compared with men, young women seemed to be more settled in the stable local wage jobs, particularly those in white-collar positions. Despite the gender difference, villagers in general continued to respect and desire the high-rank salaried jobs, such as civil servants, teachers, doctors, and those with professional skills or qualifications.

Family cooperation and gender roles

In either entrepreneurial or wage work sectors, women had played an active role in Su Village, and many women expressed a sense of self-confidence related with their earning activities. Given the prevalent dual-earner pattern, women were reluctant to give up their own jobs for their husbands' career or business, but at the same time, they were not perceived as the ideal persons to lead entrepreneurial activities. Most of the time, women valued what they could get from wage jobs, such as welfare and insurance benefits. A few dynamic women did enter the business world, but often together with their husbands, who took the lead.

Gaozhu was a confident young woman and an elder daughter in an entrepreneur's family. She was 35 years old when interviewed in 2010, and had taken the position of the village women's officer since 2007, partly because of her resourceful family background and diverse working experiences. Gaozhu's father had been the collective manager of the cotton mill (after Gubo), but Gaozhu chose not to enter her father's factory after she graduated from middle school, but joined the clothes corporation in 1992 at the age of 17 to gain her economic independence. She married a young man who was a driver in the workplace, and had her daughter at the age of 23. Gaozhu quit her factory job to work on her own schedule to take care of the baby; she rented a salesroom in the county seat and began to sell textile products together with her sister.

After spending two years in her own business, Gaozhu found that "it was too risky to run business by two women." "My sister and I were dealing with tens of thousands of yuan in transactions, and we needed to chase those who did not pay the whole amount immediately. . . . [We] were intimidated by the risk." The two sisters returned to their father's factory, the cotton mill, because the father wanted them to come back to help run the factory after it was privatized in 1998. Around the same time, Gaozhu's husband also quit his previous job and joined the management of the cotton mill. After her father retired from the leading position around 2008, Gaozhu and her husband had taken over most management tasks, while Gaozhu described her role as to support and facilitate her husband's leading position in the enterprise.

Gaozhu had been curious and brave to try out different earning opportunities and eventually returned to her family business as the second generation of an entrepreneur's family. This was partly because Su Village was industrialized in a way modeled after urban centers and dominated by big industries, and there was limited room for small businesses that were usually perceived as "manageable" by women themselves. Meanwhile, Gaozhu tried to prioritize her family roles by giving more management responsibility to her husband. Her role of women's officer was also very different from previous female village cadres like Meijing, who had embraced the ethics of self-sacrifice and hard work. Gaozhu no longer saw participation in the public sphere as empowering and honorable, but took it as a wage job. For her, public participation was not an honor, but a distraction from her own economic activities and family obligations.

Gaozhu's case was unusual because she was the daughter of an entrepreneur, and most women her age typically spent their lives as factory workers. But Gaozhu's case was representative that even though women were empowered by resources and earning capabilities, they still emphasized their family roles. This was true even in families that had no sons and had heavily invested in their daughters. For example, these families usually adopted uxorilocal marriages to enable a man to marry into the family and inherit the family property together with their daughter. Among the 46 couples in the sample, 12 of them had adopted uxorilocal marriage for themselves or for their children (26 percent). Among the related respondents, three were men who married into the wives' families, four were women who had a married-in husband, and five of them had a married-in son-in-law.

At first glance, it seemed that a daughter gained an equal status with a son in inheriting the family property. If the family had only daughters, the parents would not want to "lose" them when they got married, and via uxorilocal marriage, they would be able to not only retain their daughter but also gain a son-in-law, and have the grandchild adopt the family's surname. In general, the family estate could be inherited by a daughter if she had a married-in husband. In cases of private businesses, the parents would not rely on only a daughter to be in charge; they would prefer that she have a husband to work together with her. To some extent, the son-in-law was a substitute for the son.

But still, women enjoyed more resources and power over time given the adapting marriage practices and the declining fertility rate. Families in Su Village experienced a fast decrease in the number of children (Table 4.3). Meanwhile, many young women had chosen to have fewer children, which could lessen their parenting burden. Meanwhile, the decline of fertility was related with greater gender equality between boys and girls in receiving education investment using national statistics (Wu, Ye, & He, 2014). Such a relationship could be particularly strong in areas where women have more opportunities to translate their human capital into economic returns. In Su Village, women had been recognized for their comparable earning capabilities in the local wage sector compared with men, and the division of labor between young couples seemed to be more egalitarian over time.

Meiya was also the only daughter of the family. Although her family did not ask her husband to marry into the wife's family, Meiya remained in close connection with her parents. Because her husband was a sales manager working in another city, Meiya moved back to stay with her parents together with her daughter when her husband was away. Because Meiya was busy with her own work, her mother provided crucial help with housework and taking care of the child. Fortunately, Meiya and her daughter could have lunch at the workplace and at school, so Meiya's mother only needed to cook dinner for the whole family. Still, Meiya felt that it was unfair for her mother to work continuously outside home and at home with almost no "leisure" time, while Meiya's mother still hoped to free her daughter from the double burden and have a different life.

To some extent, young women like Meiya rediscovered the glory of working outside home, not under the state ideology or the collective patronage, but through cultivating their personal qualifications and climbing up career ladders. Backed up by her own career development, Meiya insisted on a more egalitarian sharing of household responsibilities between her and her husband. When her husband came back for a short stay at home, Meiya suggested that he should also help with household chores, and she proudly claimed that her husband could

Table 4.3 Number of children in the sample in Su Village

Mother born in	0		1		2		3		4		5 and more		Total	Average
1920s							50%		50%				2	3.5
1930s					50%		50%						2	2.5
1940s			27%		73%								11	1.7
1950s			80%		20%								10	1.2
1960s			75%		25%								4	1.25
1970s			88%		12%								8	1.1
1980s	40%		60%										5	0.6
Total	2	5%	24	57%	13	31%	2	5%	1	2%	0	0%	42	

Note: The number of children is missing for 4 of 46 cases, so there are 42 valid cases. If the mother's age is missing, the father's age is used as an approximate. The blank cells are used to refer to 0%.

cook as well. Such egalitarian statements were found for some young couples, in which the wife earned a similar or higher income than her husband.

As such, different generations of men and women had different experiences and expectations about their economic contributions and family roles. Old women had frequently divided their time between factory work, farming, and domestic work. Young people entered the labor market when the family farming tasks had been greatly reduced and when local industries provided great chances of job mobility. They stayed in school longer, did less housework, and had a clearer boundary of work and leisure, as found in other Chinese villages (Huang, 2011). Their claim for a more egalitarian division of labor within couples suggested a shift from "self-sacrifice" as a woman's virtue to "self-satisfaction" as an individual right. Young women were empowered by their greater earning power based on their prolonged education, but when they started to gain equal status relative to their husbands, it was usually not husbands but grandmothers who took over domestic work. In such cases, the gender equality among young spouses was achieved at the expense of the "discounted" labor of grandmothers.

In sum, marriage patterns and the family division of labor had evolved given the ample nonfarm work opportunities for both men and women outside home on the one hand, and the decline of fertility and the eagerness to have a child to inherit the family (or the business) on the other hand. Parents had invested more in children's self-development in education and careers regardless of their gender, but they still wanted a son or a daughter with a married-in husband to inherit the family. This was related with how resources were distributed within the community. Although economic development in Su Village had been built on the persisting collective legacy, the patterns of resource distribution were still largely based on households. This created a subtle context for the patriarchal and patrilineal norms in the family life to be maintained and revised.

Insiders' benefits and the new socialist countryside

The evolving patterns of marriage and inheritance reflected the importance of the insiders' benefits enjoyed by villagers regarding work, housing, and collective welfare. Based on village membership, both men and women enjoyed the privilege of obtaining local factory jobs rather easily. Regarding housing, the housing quota was distributed based on the number of households in the village, so it could be a result of division of a larger family after the adult sons took in brides and established their own families. For families that did not have sons, one of the daughters might stay with her natal family via uxorilocal marriage. Due to the benefits derived from village membership, it was more desirable for not only women but also men to marry into the village, to get access to housing and collective welfare.

Villagers used to live in self-built housing, but it was gradually replaced by the collective housing project of standard single-family houses. The project was coordinated by the village leadership and largely funded with its collective budget, in order to build "modern" compact housing neighborhoods rather than random, scattered, and self-built housing that lacked the modern infrastructures and facilities. This was meant to beautify rural living environments and was highly praised by local governments and media. Because villages could buy these single-family houses at low prices, it was considered a "privilege" for village members. To build such a compact housing community, the village had rezoned the land of different villagers' groups, designated a residential area, moved all households into the new housing neighborhood, and demolished the old housing. This was considered a more efficient way to use land under the government's call to modernize village infrastructures and construct the new socialist countryside. The housing project was initiated in 1999 and finished around 2009. It included around 430 houses, and each house cost around 260,000–300,000 yuan to build, with a floor space of 220–300 square meters. Eligible villagers only needed to pay for around half of the construction cost.

In addition to housing benefits, villagers also enjoyed other advantages, such as public goods[22] and subsidies. Within the village, the elderly received 38 yuan per month (for men above the age of 60 and women above 55); the subsidy increased to 50 yuan when in their 70s, and 60 yuan when in their 80s.[23] Some other benefits were distributed for everyone based on their village membership, "such as the 100 yuan of shopping coupons at the end of the year."[24] Some peasants still went to cadres when they could not find a job, and the village leadership would coordinate to find a position for them, such as security guard or gardener.[25] The standard outlook of villagers' houses and the neatly designed neighborhoods helped to represent the prosperity of the local economy and the "harmonious" social relations despite the emerging inequalities among villagers.

The efforts to build the new socialist countryside also meant modernization of agriculture and other economic sectors. The big-scale farming was coordinated by the village leadership, and such opportunities were often reserved for local managerial farmers and agricultural corporations that had local connections and had won the support of local governments. Similar to what happened in local industries, the agricultural corporation recruited many migrant workers to conduct the manual labor, while reserving managerial positions for locals. Despite the stratification among villagers, they in general occupied a better position in the labor market compared with migrant workers from the outside.

As the reform unfolded, the tradition of collective patronage was revised, and the employment relationship gained more importance in providing economic security. To a large extent, it was the biggest enterprises rather than the village office that provided insider benefits. After the enterprises were privatized, the village office had to rely on co-optating the most successful entrepreneurs to stabilize the local institution of welfare and economic security. At the same time, the local welfare systems were supplemented by the macro-level promotion of the new rural cooperative medical insurance system and social welfare systems, including the new rural social pension insurance system and the minimum life guarantee system of rural residents. By 2005, ninety percent of the villagers had joined the rural cooperative medical insurance system and 95 percent had joined the rural pension system.[26] These government-coordinated welfare policies were implemented with wide coverage in this area, which was partly related to the fact that villagers could rely on local governments and employers to share the costs or deposits.

As such, the employment relationship still played an important role in the villagers' access to welfare. Respondents who worked in the clothes corporation mentioned that the employer would cover 70 percent of the payment for the insurance package (including medical cost and pension), and an employee might only need to pay around 200 yuan per month (to be deducted from the wage).[27] Respondents had compared different employers to see which provided the best insurance package payments, and the generosity of employers in welfare benefits was closely related with their "ranking" in the market. From this perspective, the best jobs were those of formal government officials and professionals, and working in big corporations was better than working in small enterprises, because the former provided jobs that were more stable and had more economic security.[28] As such, not only the differences between individual positions in the workplace but also the stratification between employers mattered in shaping one's position in the labor market.

Unlike peasants in other rural areas in inland China, people in Su Village usually did not need to travel far to gain earning opportunities. This advantage was added by the emergence of the managerial, professional, and white-collar positions in local wage sectors. Some villagers did travel a lot, but they were mostly the managers or salespersons who were sent by local industries to other factory bases or sales centers. The private sector was also on the rise, but was dominated by several big, well-established enterprises, which left limited room for self-employment and small businesses. For most villagers, the mainstream employment pattern was to enter the wage sector instead of starting new ventures. Due to the persisting collective legacy in organizing economic activities, family cooperation had been less important in the economic sphere. Although some entrepreneurs did have their family members and relatives play important roles in the management teams, ordinary families only cooperated in household chores and care work. As Su Village had been modeled after big urban manufacturing centers since the early reform years given its close connections with coastal industrial and commercial centers, local people had a stronger incentive to invest in education in order to enter the big enterprises and climb up the more institutionalized career ladders, rather than relying on family accumulations as the basis of economic mobility.

As such, villagers had a strong attachment to the collective in the early reform years and then to the big employers starting in the 1990s. The importance of village membership was gradually replaced by that of the relationship with employers in an increasingly privatized rural economy. At the family level, both men and women gained more economic independence and earning power under a massive locally based transition from the farming sector to nonagricultural jobs, which was often based on their village membership and their connections with local big enterprises. Given the prevalence of "individualized" wage work, many young marrieds became dual-earner couples, which echoed the rise of "girl power" in rural areas elsewhere (Yan, 2006). With regard to the rising "girl power," Yan found that young women were empowered and took more authority away from the mothers-in-law, without challenging the role of their husbands. In Su Village, the rise of women's employment similarly avoided the direct conflict with that of men, with women's concentration in locally based white-collar jobs and men's overrepresentation as managers and salespersons traveling to other places. In this process, both local men and women had played an active role particularly in the wage sectors, but the gender gap remained and was reinterpreted in the naturalized divisions of labor when career ladders in big enterprises were institutionalized. As such, the ample earning opportunities were parallel with the continuing and revised forms of gender inequalities and segregation. Meanwhile, many old women took over the domestic responsibilities to free young women to join the labor market and develop their careers. The career duties and prospects for young local women had become good excuses for them to spend less time on family obligations, but it was usually grandmothers rather than husbands who were willing to fill in this gap.

In sum, the seemingly ample opportunities of employment and career development for both men and women came with a price. The general willingness of old generations of women to help young couples in family responsibilities was partly due to the greater upward mobility that young women faced in big enterprises, and partly because of the flexible marriage patterns in which they might provide help to their own daughters. These young women might be the only daughters – their parents had invested heavily in their educations and wished to see them succeed in their careers. Unlike what Yan (2006) found for the rising girl power – that young women took authority away from old women – young women in Su Village often felt that they owed a lot to their mothers or mothers-in-law. As the patrilocal patterns had been challenged by the low fertility rate and the rising values of daughters at home in Su Village, the intergenerational competition between different generations of women was less salient than in other rural areas. Rather, the gender gap in employment trends was to some extent reduced by the intergenerational division of labor within the family.

Notes

1 Interview with Xiaofeng, 2003.
2 The official website of the village.
3 Grain City Bureau of Statistics. 2007. *Statistic Report of Economic and Social Development, Grain City, 2006* (2006nian Grain City guominjingji he shehuifazhan tongji gongbao). Retrieved September 28, 2016 from the website of Grain City Bureau of Statistics.
4 Jiangsu Bureau of Statistics. 2007. *Statistic Report of Economic and Social Development, Jiangsu Province, 2006 (Jiangsu sheng 2006nian guomin jingji he shehuifazhan tongji gongbao)*. Retrieved September 28, 2016 from www.jssb.gov.cn/jstj/djgb/qsndtjgb/200703/t20070305_83144.htm
5 White Town Archive Compilation Committee. 2002. *White Township Archive.* Nanjing: Jiangsu Renmin Press, pp. 137–138 (pseudonym used for the town).
6 Ibid. Interview with Pingfan, 2003. A news report for the village (website) retrieved August 10, 2016 (not provided to protect the confidentiality of respondents).

7 Interview with Baokang, 2005; Guozhen, 2005; Meiya, 2010.
8 Jiangsu Provincial Government Document [2013] No 113. Retrieved March 4, 2017 from www.jiangsu.gov.cn/jsgov/tj/bgt/201309/t20130923_400467.html
9 Interview with Jinghua, 2004; Weidong, 2005; Zhigang, 2010.
10 Interview with Jinghua, 2004.
11 Interview with Bingyuan, 2005.
12 Interview with Xueying, 2010.
13 Interview with Weidong, 2005; Bingyuan, 2005.
14 Interview with Jianxin, 2004.
15 Interview with Zhoujian, 2010.
16 In addition to collective organizational links, the socialist ideological egalitarian norm, including that of gender equality, as well as the practical concerns of choosing the most capable workers, also played a role in the recruitment process.
17 Interview with Jianxin, 2010.
18 Ibid.
19 There are five cases in which education information of both spouses is missing, which are excluded from the calculation of percentage of different education groups.
20 There are 24 cases in which education information for children is missing or not applicable, and the percentage is calculated based on the 22 valid cases.
21 Interview with Liu, 2010.
22 Public goods included services or facilities such as the village clinic and the activity room for the elderly, which was rebuilt in 2006.
23 Interview with Jinghua, 2003; Pingfan, 2003, Weiming, 2004.
24 Interview with Pingfan, 2003.
25 Interview with Liu, 2005.
26 Interview with Weidong, 2005.
27 Interview with Linquan, 2010. The insurance package payment was divided between the employer and the employee by certain proportions. In the case of some other employers, both the employer and the employee paid less because the employer chose to enroll their employees in a lower class of insurance category. See interview with Wuyu, 2010.
28 Interview with Fengdan, 2010.

References

Fei, X. (1983, September 21). *Xiaochengzhen, dawenti (Small towns, big issues)*. Paper presented at Jiangsusheng xiaochengzhen yanjiu taolunhui (Symposium on Studies of Small Towns in Jiangsu Province), Nanjing, China.

Huang, Y. (2011). Labour, leisure, gender and generation: The organization of "wan" and the notion of "gender equality" in contemporary rural China. In T. Jacka & S. Sargeson (Eds.), *Women, gender and rural development in China* (pp. 49–70). Cheltenham, UK: Edward Elgar Publishing Ltd.

Murphy, R. (2002). *How migrant labor is changing rural China*. Cambridge: Cambridge University Press.

Oi, J. C. (1992). Fiscal reform and the economic foundations of local state corporatism in China. *World Politics*, 45(1), 99–126.

Su, M. Z. (2009). *China's rural development policy: Exploring the "new socialist countryside"*. Boulder, CO: First Forum Press.

Wu, X., Ye, H., & He, G. G. (2014). Fertility decline and women's status improvement in China. *Chinese Sociological Review*, 46(3), 3–25.

Yan, Y. (2006). Girl power: Young women and the waning of patriarchy in rural north China. *Ethnology*, 45(2), 105–124.

5 Han Village

Urban dream, tied migration, and male bonding

Han Village is located within the administration territory of Baoding in the middle of Hebei Province in northern China. Han Village is under the jurisdiction of Ying County, a rural county in the northwest of the municipality. Ying County has been a "poverty county (*pinkunxian*)" in Hebei Province with a low population density compared with other parts of the province. The northwest and middle parts of the county are mountainous, and the plain concentrates in its eastern part. Han Village is located in the southeastern part of the county, with a combination of mountain and plain areas. The village is 150 kilometers from Beijing, and 220 kilometers to the provincial capital, Shijiazhuang. With its location about in the middle between the two big cities, it is about three hours' drive to either one. At the same time, this area is still characterized by mountainous landscape, a low population density, and a mix of different ethnic groups.

Han village belongs to a Manchu and Hui Ethnic Autonomous township, in which the Han ethnic group counts for 79.7 percent in its population, Manchu counts for 15.3 percent, and Hui counts for 4.7 percent.[1] During the field visits to Han Village, Han and Manchu were still the two largest ethnic groups, and unlike the many surnames Han people had in the village, Manchu people mostly concentrated under four big surnames. Meanwhile, intermarriage between ethnic groups was common. The most common marriage was the intermarriage between Manchu and Han ethnic groups, more frequently observed than other types of match. Partly due to the intermingling between ethnic groups, all couples in the village had been allowed to have two children,[2] even under the tight government control in the era of strict family planning policies.

The field visits were carried out during 2007, 2008, 2009, 2010, and 2011. The interviewed cases include 65 couples: for 12 of them only the husband was interviewed, for 27 of them only the wife was interviewed, and for the remaining 26 couples, both the husband and the wife were interviewed. In total, there were 91 respondents, including 38 men and 53 women. For the couples, the husband's ages ranged from 25 to 72, and the wife's ages ranged from 28 to 76 at the time of investigation. Among respondents, there were three current village leaders at the time of investigation: the party secretary, who was Manchu, the vice secretary, who was Han; and the village council head, who was Manchu.

Han village had around 312 households and a population of around 1,315.[3] The village is divided into eight villagers' groups (or teams). More than half of the land was located on mountain slopes where irrigation was difficult, while people established several quarry sites in mountains to get stones for roadwork, construction, and other uses. Although respondents mentioned their material living conditions had been greatly improved under economic reform, it still lagged in basic infrastructure and industries. The annual income per capita of the village increased from 2,675 yuan in 2002 to around 4,000 yuan in 2010,[4] still a little lower than the county average of around 5,000 yuan and the provincial average of 5,958 yuan for rural residents in 2010.[5] The village was also included in the promotion of rural medical insurance and social welfare systems. Local people found the new rural cooperative medical insurance system a necessary tool to handle risks in life, but they were less interested in enrolling in the new rural social pension insurance system. For the minimum life guarantee system of rural residents, there were around 62 villagers received the minimum living allowance (*dibao*), which was around 50 yuan per month.

Agricultural activities had evolved together with market reforms and rural life cycles. Since agricultural land was contracted to individual families in 1980–1981, individual holding of land had remained dominant. The collective still had some small farms and orchards, to be rented to peasants to generate some limited budget for the collective. Some individual households had also subleased part of their land to others, but there was no large-scale managerial farming by cooperatives or mechanized agricultural enterprises. Growing mainly wheat, corn, peanut, soybean, and sometimes cotton, farming became less labor-intensive but meanwhile not profitable enough to support a family. In the recent decades, the village had relied on its labor migration to urban centers as a major source of income. But for local industries and businesses, neither the village leadership nor rural households had sufficient resources to develop ventures that had sustainable market efficiency and competitiveness. Despite a desire to "explore the external world," most migrant workers returned to the village and resumed the rural life cycles eventually.

Farming: declined investment and increasing flexibility

After the collective land was redistributed to families in 1980 and 1981, the agricultural system had been dominated by individual farming rather than managerial farming in Han Village. In the early reform years, the farms were collectively adjusted within the team every several years according to the changing family demographic structures. But such adjustments were terminated when the new policy of "no change in 30 years"[6] was legalized in 2003 to stabilize land tenures and to encourage investment in farms.

In Han Village, agricultural production had been constrained by the mountainous landscape. The hilly land was mostly located on mountain slopes in the southern part of the village, mainly relying on rainfall for water supply. With an egalitarian principle of land distribution, most families had a combination of hilly land (*podi*, usually the dryland) and irrigated farming land (*shuijiaodi*). In 1989 the village had total farming land of 2325.8 mu, in which dryland accounted for 1263 mu, irrigated land for 721.3 mu, and vegetable land for around 7.5 mu. Other than that, the village had around 50.1 mu of orchard and 64.3 mu of forest.[7] In 2008, village cadres estimated the total arable land amount was 1755 mu, but the well-irrigated remained to be a bit less than 800 mu.[8] The decrease in the farmland mainly occurred to dryland, which was considered less fertile and of "less worth" in agricultural terms, partly due to reforestation and partly because of the expansion of orchards, quarries, and other land uses. In 2009, each person had around 1.2 to 1.3 mu of land.[9] Although there had been less farmland for every villager on average over time, the amount of irrigated land (or the best quality land) had been relatively stable.

Peasants had tended to grow on hilly dryland one season of corn in a year, supplemented by wheat, peanut, soybean, sorghum, or sweet potato, and the two-season cropping of wheat and corn was only possible for the well-irrigated land. The conventional cropping patterns had once been challenged in the Maoist era with an inappropriate imposition of overcultivation and even grain-growing in the locality, and such efforts failed due to the limits imposed by natural endowments. Since the households were reinstated as the major units of agricultural production, the peasants' motivations to invest in family farms had helped to increase agricultural productivity, but people recognized that extensive labor input did not help to inflate productivity that was constrained by the natural "giving."[10] In a typical extended family with three or four adult laborers, the average area of family farms was around 5 to 6 mu, but usually there were only one or two persons working on the farm. Peasants began to detach themselves from land, not in a form of outsourcing their land but reducing labor investment in land.

Among respondents, it occurred frequently that the agricultural tasks were "mainly done by the wife" (37 percent among the couples who reported their farming situations), followed by "mainly done by both spouses" (26 percent), and then "mainly done by neither spouses" (23 percent). This categorization of "mainly done by whom" was due to the fact that respondents often moved back and forth between farm and off-farm work, and few had completely moved out of farming. Table 5.1 shows that the labor investment in agriculture was related with the amount and quality of land. For the categories in which farming was mainly done by the husband (14 percent) or done by both the husband and the wife (26 percent), the families had a higher average amount of land per capita to farm (1.99 mu and 1.24 mu, respectively). For the category in which farming was done by both spouses, the family also had the highest percentage of well-irrigated land on average (82 percent). As such, the family's labor investment was responsive to the amount and the presence of "good" land, and peasants adjusted the labor intensiveness in the farming sector as required by land qualities and quantities and stimulated by the expected outputs.

The "feminization of agriculture" was more common for couples in their 40s and 50s (born in the 1950 and 1960s) but less so for others. For the older and younger cohorts, it was more likely that farming was shared by both spouses or

Table 5.1 Family farming patterns and access to land in the sample in Han Village

Farming mainly done by	Percent	Land per capita (mu)	Percent irrigated land (average)	Grow trees N	Y	-1940s	1950s	1960s	1970s	1980s-
						The couple born in				
Husband	14%	1.99	62%	6	2	25%	20%	7%		
Wife	37%	1.12	60%	17	4	8%	50%	60%	14%	
Husband and wife	26%	1.24	82%	12	3	17%	25%	33%	43%	
Neither	23%	0.92	75%	12	1	50%	5%		43%	100%
Total	57			48	9	12	20	15	7	3

Note: Information of farm composition and labor division is available for 57 couples in the sample of 65 couples. If the spouses were not born in the same decade, the average age of the spouses is used to approximate their cohort. The blank cells are used to refer to 0%.

taken by neither spouse. The pattern of "men work and women plough" (Judd, 2002, p. 34) was common among the middle age group, in which men were typically working outside and leaving farms to their wives. Older generations were either returning to farms or too old to work at all in the field, and the farming task had been passed on to other family members. Younger generations were more active in working outside the home and less interested in farming. But for quite some of them, the proportion of farming was mainly done by "both spouses" (43 percent for the cohort born in the 1970s, higher than that of "either spouse"). This was different from other cohorts, in which it was more common that farming was done by one spouse, more often the wife. This could happen when there were no other family members to "free" them from farm work, such as after they split from the extended family and had their own piece of land. But even for the young cohorts, if farming was mainly done by "either spouse," the farming tasks still fell more often on the wife (although this percentage was lower than the middle-age women). But as suggested by the high proportion of "farming mainly done by neither spouse," these young couples were likely to have left farms to their parents or in-laws.

Among middle-age women who showed a stronger tendency of the "feminization of agriculture," quite some respondents suggested that they willingly "freed" their children from farming tasks. These women had blended farming into sideline and domestic work, but it had been rare for them to multitask in direct income-generating activities due to the underdevelopment of local industries. Most of them grew vegetables and raised pigs and chickens only for self-consumption. There were only four households that specialized in livestock raising, and half of them had quit due to the limited market profit margin.

Recently, some women began to make gloves and shoe insoles to earn some cash income. But unlike the sideline needlework in Bei Village that had been cherished as an important source of income before market reforms, such home-based industries rose recently as a leisure-time activity to earn pocket money for women who could not go outside to work with their family obligations. Because Han Village had little craftsmanship and sideline traditions, such sideline jobs only arose after the agents moved from the eastern coastal areas to the inland areas to seek cheap and "surplus" laborers. Such home-based work had thrived in coastal areas but lost its attractiveness due to rural industrialization, but in Han Village, such home-based earning opportunities were still observed among the "left-behind" women (14 cases among the 65 interviewed families). It was usually taken by women in their 30s and 40s who were less preoccupied by farm work than the older generations but were less competitive in the labor market than the younger and nimble girls.

A few women were the exceptions who extended farming to home-based business. One example was Wenyu (aged 46 when interviewed in 2009), who benefited from the family's resource and manpower. Wenyu and her husband, Juzhi, had high school educations, which was outstanding in their generation (Juzhi is one year older than Wenyu). As an educated and confident young woman, Wenyu tried to become a tailor and a teacher, but both careers had limited prospects at that time in an inland village. She got married at the age of 24 and began to work in the fields with her in-laws, and her husband Juzhi moved to the quarry and other businesses. Together with her in-laws, Wenyu rented around 40 mu of mountainous land from the collective in addition to farming the 7 mu of the family land in the late 1980s. Around the same time, she ran a food processing factory with her father-in-law, which was to process the agricultural outputs into wheat powder or fine products for villagers. Wenyu had to rely on her mother-in-law to take care of her two toddler children in order to concentrate on her farming and business tasks. However, such family workshops had declined in the 2000s, due to the competition from urban enterprises and external capital.

Most families that were less resourceful often relied on the combination of migrant work and farm work by the left-behind, and peasants had relied on mutual-help social networks to fill the seasonal labor gap (Jacka, 2012). But more recently, people began to hire seasonal laborers in the harvesting season. Wenyu, who used to grow peanuts on 10 mu of land, also hired someone to "watch the land" during the non-busy season, which cost around 20 yuan a day compared with the average wage of 30–40 yuan a day in the harvesting season.[11] Although she still tended to hire someone she "trusted" and "knew well," Wenyu adapted to the calculating nature of market transactions. Under the new market logic that "people all need to make money," she chose to "give the payment right away" rather than owing a favor, as she also had no time to work in other people's fields.

The commodification of agricultural labor had two facets. Some of the laborers were employed together with harvesting machines and moved between villages to harvest whichever village's wheat ripened first and then moved on to the next village. Such "technical" labor was mainly done by men who specialized in this new business. The other laborers were local part-time agricultural workers, including quite a few middle-aged women, who had to stay in the village for their own farming obligations. Some of these laborers had been organized by local agricultural "contractors." According to Wenyu, it was easy to hire temporary help by calling an agricultural "contractor," who would send immediately the required number of laborers.

The mechanization and commodification of agricultural work had led farming to be more manageable but not more profitable. Peasants saw no hope of transforming their farms into high-yield projects such as greenhouses due to the lack of water. Seeing the limited incomes derived from the farming sector, many families had reduced labor investment, and even families like Wenyu's had returned the rented land to the village collective, and turned to grow less labor-intensive crops on their land. With villagers' declining interest in agriculture, Wenyu also closed their food-processing workshop as her in-laws got old. Both of her children attended universities and "never touched farm work," and they planned to find a job in cities after graduation. Because farming became more manageable by the left-behind, the divide between on-farm and off-farm work occurred more often between generations rather than between genders over time. But women were still more likely to be left behind if there were no parents or in-laws to help.

Given the overall decrease in labor investment in farming, peasants mentioned that they only maintained the farms at a level for self-sufficiency. For the "mountainous" land, many families chose to grow trees rather than crops. Han Village was included in the north shelter forest area, and the national strategy of environmental sustainability allowed peasants to reforest their farming land under certain conditions. Respondents suggested that they divided their crop-growing and tree-growing land to avoid "wasting labor input on the hilly land that had poor yields" and to "concentrate on cultivating the more fertile land."[12] After sending some family members to seek nonagricultural work, the families became patient in waiting for trees to grow up every three to five years, which could be sold or used as housing construction materials for the families.

Growing trees was encouraged by the flexible local implementation of central policies of promoting agriculture and protecting the environment. Both policies were accompanied by government subsidies, in addition to the removal of the agricultural tax in the mid-2000s. But to receive the subsidy to encourage reforestation and halt soil degradation, peasants needed to grow at least 15 mu of trees (about one hectare or 10,000 square meters or 2.47 acres) in principle, and it was difficult for the local small-scale tree-growing activities to meet this standard. In fact, village cadres applied "staple food subsidies" (*liangshi butie*) to all farms regardless of whether peasants grew wheat or trees on it. Such practices were convenient and practical for a locality with fragmented pieces of land and moderate levels of yields. Such flexibility was used by village cadres as a way to serve the community. The village leadership had received complaints as being incapable of supporting industrialization or providing welfare benefits, and such flexible implementation of policies was seen by cadres as a way to sooth the discontents of villagers. The options of growing trees and other crops enabled peasants to use farms for diverse purposes to support themselves in the market while ensuring self-sufficiency.

The evolvement of the farming sector, together with the combination of pro-agricultural policies and tree-growing practices, made farming tasks more manageable and to some extent freed young people to seek alternative employment. But many respondents still suggested farming as an important fallback position. Although peasants did not see a chance of getting rich by farming and receiving government subsidies, peasants had strong incentives to keep one foot in the farming sector. It was still difficult for peasants to settle down in cities, and the presence of the rural base helped to reduce the anxiety of losing off-farm jobs.

"Going to Beijing" or "going up to the mountain"

Compared with the more industrialized coastal rural areas, villagers in Han Village relied more heavily on migrant work in urban centers, due to the under-development of local rural industries. Men's migrant work had existed in the 1960s and 1970s but rose rapidly beginning in the 1980s along with the massive development and redevelopment projects in cities, as well as construction projects of roads, rivers, and highways. Beijing remained the most important destination, and "going to Beijing" was often a term referring to migrant work. Among respondents, men remained more represented in migrant employment with their dominance in construction work, but that of women also increased in recent decades with their concentration in manufacturing and service work.

In addition to "going to Beijing," "going up to the mountain" was another common choice among male peasants to carry and transport stones for the quarries to meet the demand of mushrooming construction and roadwork projects nearby. Compared with local work "in the mountains," migrant work in urban areas usually paid better, but villagers sometimes felt it too tedious and costly to work and live away from home. Compared with the harsh working conditions of migrant work, people with local jobs could return home every day and "eat well." Such jobs were usually paid by the actual working days, were relatively flexible, and attracted male laborers who were either taking a rest from migrant work or were too old to seek external opportunities, including a retired primary school teacher and a former village cadre in the sample. They did not feel discomfort or shame for picking up a less prestigious job, and felt satisfied as long as they could make money.

However, local work alone could not meet major expenses in peasants' life cycles: raising children, building housing to attract a bride to marry in, and establishing new families and raising the next generation. Migrant work was often "necessary" to earn cash income to deal with the life-course burdens. Most families borrowed money to finance housing construction and marriage expenses and then paid it back in the following years with their wage income. The length of migrant work was then contingent on family structures, such as how many sons the family had. For example, Xuemin, a 51-year-old man when interviewed in 2007, spent only a few years in migrant work because he had only one son. In the 1980s, he followed other villagers to Beijing and worked in several short-term jobs such as trading vegetables, and his wife stayed behind to farm and raise chickens and pigs. After accumulating some savings, Xuemin returned to the village to build a new house. He had been engaged in local jobs of "going up to the mountain" and transporting stones for the quarries since then, and the flexible work schedule was compatible with the family's housing construction plan. Even after he returned from migrant work, Xuemin still left most farm work to his wife, who also grew vegetables and raised chickens.

At the time of the interview in 2007, their 24-year-old son was to get married within a month, and their 26-year-old daughter had married into a nearby village. The family had spent around 80,000 yuan on housing construction and would spend another 40,000 yuan for marriage expenses for their son, which would leave the family with a debt of 30,000 yuan, mostly borrowed from relatives. Still, the couple was happy that their "life goal" was almost done, and Xuemin saw a hope of paying back the debt in three years with the income from his local work. "Transporting one cart is worth 1 yuan, and I earn around 40 yuan a day, because I do not work as hard as those who earn 80 yuan a day." Some other men, however, joked that they "cannot retire until finishing the task of our lives." "Even if you are 80, you cannot call yourself old and cannot give up working when your son is not yet married," they commented, and envied the "fortunate" guys who could "retire at the age of 50 and 'relax.'"[13]

Centering on housing construction, men often adjusted their work choices accordingly and moved back and forth between local work and migrant work, whereas their wives usually stayed to farm. Several men who had two or three sons continued their migrant work sometimes into their 40s and 50s. Meanwhile, young people in these families also started working at an early age, while their limited education qualifications enabled them to find only low-paid manual jobs with little potential for career development. Quite often, both fathers and sons needed to do migrant work together to finance housing construction and marriage.

Some families adopted a new division of labor, where parents constructed housing at home and children left to earn and send wages to support the continuous investment in housing, because of the greater earning potential of young people in construction and manufacturing sectors and the declining competitiveness of old people in the labor market. Wencai, a 58-year-old man when interviewed in 2010, had three sons who were 27, 30, and 33 years old at that time. The family rebuilt their old house in 1990 and planned to build three more because "girls do not want to marry into a family with no good housing." The eldest son became a migrant worker after finishing middle school, and so did the two younger brothers afterward. The first new house was built during 1997–2000, just in time for the eldest son to get engaged. In 2002 Wencai started to build a new house for the second son, but Wencai fell severely ill in the middle. Wencai's wife had to borrow from relatives to deal with the dual burden of housing and medical expenses, and barely finished the construction in 2003 to allow the second son to get married. When the youngest son was to get married, the family had no financial capability to build another house. The old couple renovated their old house for the youngest son in 2005, and they continued to live together after the elder sons split their own families from the extended family. The old couple felt sorry for their youngest son, as "the third daughter-in-law spent the least amount of money [to get married], around 10,000 yuan [compared with 20,000 yuan for each of the elder daughters-in-law]," and indicated that this house would be inherited by the young couple.

As suggested by the local saying "the youngest (son) is the most miserable," the family coordination of migration and investment involved conflicts of individual interests. Parents might have exhausted their resources to build housing for elder sons, and after they established their own families, the elder sons were less willing to support their younger siblings to get married. Meanwhile, as a common practice, parents often ended up living with the youngest son after the family split, and the old couple often helped in farming and domestic work for the young couple. This was true in Wencai's case. His youngest son, Juhai, was fortunate to form a free-love marriage with the reduced marriage cost, "because with no housing, no people would introduce their daughters to you."[14] Juhai had worked in Beijing as a construction worker and then as a security guard for some years when he met his wife, Xiaohui, who was from a neighboring village and also worked in Beijing as a salesgirl in a curtain shop. Compared with the matches of the elder siblings based on local social networks, the young couple "found each other by themselves," getting to know each other on the bus to commute to Beijing. They got married in 2005 and had a daughter in 2007, and Xiaohui resumed her migrant work when her daughter was only three months old. With the help of grandparents, the young couple could move back and forth between the village and Beijing to do migrant work.

Xiaohui was among the young women who spent extended time in migrant work. Similar to men, women's migrant work also increased in the 1980s, but was still lower than their representation in local jobs, and their migrant work often terminated after they had children. Take respondents who were born in the 1970s, for example: women were active in both local and migrant work in their 20s, as were men. When they reached their 30s, women's employment illustrated a decline in migrant work and an increase in local work. In contrast, men had a more even distribution between local and migrant work over life stages. Compared with this cohort, older women's concentration in local work was more salient. This was rooted in the gendered division that men did migrant work to earn housing expenses and marriage costs, and women stayed to farm. As farming became more manageable over time, women who were left behind began to explore diverse local employment opportunities, such as helping in fields, cooking for quarries, or making gloves. The wage jobs of younger cohorts were more "migration oriented," with the help of their parents or in-laws to free them from farming tasks. Such generational differences are summarised in Table 5.2.

As men's engagement in migrant work was contingent on the family's economic needs, women's migrant work was more dependent on family structures. Living with her in-laws, Xiaohui never worried about the family farm. The couple migrated together to Beijing and came back once several months, and sometimes they stayed at home for a longer time when they could not find jobs, such as when the city tried to reduce the congestion during the 2008 Beijing

Table 5.2 Local and migrant wage workers in the sample in Han Village

Born in	Gender	Number	<20 (the age of respondents)		20-30		30-40		40-50		50-60		>60	
			L	M	L	M	L	M	L	M	L	M	L	M
1930s	M	3		33%		33%		33%	33%					
	F	1											100%	
1940s	M	7	29%		29%	14%	29%	14%	29%	29%	14%	29%	14%	14%
	F	3									33%		33%	
1950s	M	20	20%	5%	35%	25%	40%	25%	35%	25%	25%	25%		15%
	F	17	6%		12%		12%	6%	12%	6%	12%	6%		
1960s	M	19		11%	32%	5%	37%	5%	53%	11%		37%	/	/
	F	16		6%	19%	19%	25%	19%	25%	33%	/	/	/	/
1970s	M	9		44%	56%	33%	33%	33%	/	33%	/	/	/	/
	F	10			20%	30%	50%	50%	/	/	/	/	/	/
1980s	M	4		50%	50%	75%	/	/	/	/	/	/	/	/
	F	2		50%	50%	50%	/	/	/	/	/	/	/	/
Total		111												

L = local work, M = migrant work.

Note: Among 65 couples, there were 62 men and 49 women (111 in total) who had complete working trajectory information. "/" means "not applicable" and the blank cells are used to refer to 0%.

Olympics. Despite these disruptions, both spouses had relied on migrant work as the major source of income. But for the two elder brothers of Juhai, because they did not have the help from parents in farming and domestic work, their wives had to be stay-at-home mothers when the husbands left for construction and manufacturing work in cities. The wives recently took home-based work in sewing for shoe insoles and gloves, which only resulted in 20–30 yuan per day compared with the regular daily wage of around 100 yuan for migrant work. The different situations of Xiaohui and her sisters-in-law suggested that women might be empowered or disadvantaged by splitting into small families. Although the rising independence of young people from extended families was celebrated as gaining authority from old generations (Yan, 2006), the presence of grandparents could also facilitate young people, particularly women, to work outside home.

Meanwhile, the effect of family structures was still moderated by other factors, either economic or ideological. Due to the local economic structure that heavily relied on the construction and transportation sectors, there were more "men's jobs" (physically more demanding and involving traveling alone) than "women's work." Jobs of "going to Beijing" were often considered too far away for women with family obligations and those of "going up to the mountain" were too harsh and risky for women. In ideological terms, women's migrant work was constrained by the common belief that "the external world is chaotic (*waimian tailuan*)," which was mentioned by several male respondents. From this perspective, local work and home-based sideline activities were favored because women were likely to be "protected" or watched by family members. In recent decades, young women became more active in migrant work in their 20s (in the sample, 19 percent for women born in the 1960s, 30 percent for those born in the 1970s, 50 percent for those born in the 1980s, see Table 5.2), but few of them extended migrant work into their 30s. Meanwhile, women seemed to have a greater chance of continuing their migrant work if they conducted tied-migration together with their husbands, which was considered "safer."

These "migrant couples" were among the young generation who had different aspirations given their greater exposure to the labor market. Unlike older generations who had framed their life goals as "marrying their sons" and letting children start work at an early age, they were more interested in "sending children to receive better education" as another life goal. Tied migration was perceived to protect women from "corrupting" market forces, but unlike conventional tied migration, both spouses had their own jobs: Juhai continued his job as a security guard and Xiaohui had tried new jobs in nail salons and restaurants in recent years. This also made it difficult for them to bring their daughter with them, but they considered such separation necessary in order to prepare for a better future for their daughter. Like other young people in similar situations, they did not expect to be migrant workers their whole lives and wished to save money to start their own business. However, the savings from migrant work was often too limited to afford startup costs for businesses, and the efforts of becoming one's own boss frequently failed due to the lack of family resources.

Quarry and transportation business: male bonding and disputes

Respondents mentioned 20 private businesses that had been conducted by villagers: 6 of them were quarries, 7 in transportation, and the rest were food stands, retail stores, barbershops, clinics, and other businesses. Many of the villagers had moved between different jobs and ventures, and half of the businesses had been closed at the time of our investigation. These ventures were ranked by villagers regarding profitability and prestige: quarries were at the top of the hierarchy with around 20–30 employees and around 1 million yuan of annual output; transportation was the second; small stores were the third, which generated an annual profit of around 10,000 yuan, similar to the income level of migrant workers. Businesses of quarries and transportation were often regarded as men's business, whereas women were more likely to be in charge of businesses on smaller scales, such as stores and barbershops.

There had been a few collective enterprises, but all of them were closed or collapsed. The biggest township enterprise that had provided opportunities to peasants for local wage jobs was closed in 1983, and the local state had given up the trials to support local entrepreneurial activities since then. Compared with coastal areas, private businesses rose in Han Village when the reform was further unfolded, and there was little need for the village leadership to protect or intervene in the operation of private businesses. The local state, as quarry owners complained, played mainly a routine role to collect the permission fee for quarries to develop natural resources. Due to the large demand of stones and construction materials in the recent development projects nearby, the government had tightened controls to run quarries in the mountainous areas to prevent the over-development of natural resources, and it now cost more than 100,000 yuan to get the permit to operate a quarry. On a contract basis, the quarry owner needed to renew the permit with the village leadership every three years.

As such, connections (*menlu*) were an important factor to facilitate the establishment of businesses. Juzhi was among the first ones to lease a quarry site together with four partners. Juzhi was well connected in local social networks partly because his two elder brothers were cadres in the provincial and prefecture governments, and he had moved between different economic opportunities eagerly, from renting collective land, running small business, to operating the quarry. He began to run the quarry in the 1980s, much earlier than many other quarry owners, who began their businesses in the 1990s. To some extent, the effect of connections was related with the "power persistence" theory (Guang & Zheng, 2005) that people who were close to local cadres or had organizational links could still benefit from a semi-redistributive power in local entrepreneurship. By pooling together economic resources among partners, Juzhi and the other four families made good income from the quarry and had become the first ones to get rich. In 2002, Juzhi participated in the village election and competed with another quarry owner to be the village party secretary. His success was largely related to his networking resources and economic standing, which was related to a potential to contribute to the community.

In such businesses, connections were also used to mobilize resources and form partnerships. An ordinary family usually could not afford to invest in running quarries, and cooperation usually occurred in a small social circle of men who were trusted by each other. These men usually represented their households in applying for small loans that were designed for groups of peasant households. As a group, they were eligible to apply for a startup loan to run a small business, which was promoted by local governments as a measure of poverty alleviation.

In businesses of quarries and transportation that were considered "men's work," men played a dominant role in pooling investments within big families and between relatives and friends. Such businesses might also involve their wives or daughters-in-law, who helped to run errands. Xingmei, a 42-year-old woman when interviewed in 2007, joined the quarry established by her father-in-law in 1991 at the age of 26 after being married for 3 years.

The quarry used to involve other households, but other partners withdrew from the business at that time, and only Xingmei's father-in-law renewed the contract for the following three years. As such, the old couple had relied on their eldest son and daughter-in-law to help with the operation of the quarry: Xingmei's husband helped to operate the machines at the quarry site, and Xingmei helped to watch the quarry site and manage daily payments for employees. She left her two young children to her mother-in-law, who stayed at home to "cook for the family." Xingmei usually finished lunch early to go to the quarry site, so that her father-in-law could come home to have lunch and take a nap. Accordingly to Xingmei, if they could work with resourceful parents, young people would not be eager for an early family separation.

After running the quarry for three years, Xingmei's family was joined by other partners to renew the contract in 1994. The collaboration continued until 1999, when Xingmei's father-in-law fell ill, and the household quit the quarry business in that year. Because the quarry business involved long-term investment in machines and considerable debt burden, the family moved to a less "risky" business in transportation. Xingmei and her husband acquired the wheel loader from the quarry, which cost them 180,000 yuan and for which they were still in debt. The couple began to use the wheel loader for transportation and earn smaller income, but with smaller market risks compared with their previous quarry business.

In some other quarries, the collaboration occurred between brothers or brothers-in-law. Quite often, the "brotherhood" bonding was emphasized given the male dominance in quarry and transportation businesses. Such male bonding also occurred among men who were not real brothers or brothers-in-law, and the "brotherhood" could be informally contracted with a ceremonial celebration among men. Haitao, a 27-year-old man when interviewed in 2008, was one of the 13 sworn brothers in Han Village. Having grown up in a single-parent family, Haitao dropped out of middle school at the age of 16 and went to Beijing to work in a construction site with fellow villagers in 1997. He soon realized that migrant work did not lead to career development and joined a three-month training program in a vocational school in 1999, hoping to be a cook to help his father, who used to have a restaurant in the county seat but failed in the business.

Since this time, his networking with his "good brothers" began to be helpful. Haitao first followed one of his friends to the city of Baoding to run a restaurant, and one year later, he joined one of his sworn brothers in the business of drilling wells in another county. This sworn brother had a rich father, who bought 4 drilling machines for his son, while at that time there were no more than 100 drilling machines in the whole county. With great market opportunities, Haitao and his sworn brother traveled around different counties to drill wells for around two years before the market got saturated. Haitao earned 20,000 yuan in two years, which made him one of the richest young men in the village in 2003. In the following years he moved to Hainan together with his uncle and cousin, where they joined a friend in his real estate business. Recently, Haitao bought a van with two other sworn brothers, taking passengers between the village and Beijing.

In the businesses of quarries, transportation, and drilling wells, the owners and partners were usually male, although the female family members might also be involved to handle logistics, manage payments, and collect tickets. For both practical and ideological reasons, men were the ones who were perceived to be better connected to run such businesses and to handle the risks and dangers of running them. There were a few businesses in which women were in charge, such as two small stores, a barbershop, a clinic, and a food stand. One of the stores was run by Haitao's wife, Yue, who was the only daughter and inherited the store from her parents. Haitao regarded the store as the best choice for his wife, a flexible and comfortable job with a reasonable income of 8,000 yuan a year. Yue could earn around the same if she became a migrant worker, but the young couple considered it not worthwhile to travel far and be separated. According to Haitao, such small shops were considered a good "woman's job," and he avoided being involved in them.

Although "men's businesses" were larger and regarded as more prestigious, they were often constrained by their limited resources and faced various difficulties in further development. The local quarries prospered in the 1990s due to the market demand for stone materials given the construction of roads and railways nearby, but many owners worried that it would not last long. Due to market fluctuations, it was sometimes difficult to sell stones, and the profit margin for the quarry industry had shrunk in the 2000s. In 2009, Juzhi and his partners withdrew from the direct operation of the quarry, outsourced it to an entrepreneur from Zhejiang, and earned a stable rent of 50,000 yuan a year without worrying about the market situations. Around the same time, several other local quarries were taken over by outsiders. Compared with external competitors, local quarries were small, were run with pooled resources from multiple families, and were vulnerable to market risks. The "outside" enterprises that took over the local quarries were more "professional, equipped with better machines," and were able to invest millions of yuan even with market fluctuations.[15] In contrast, local businesses were smaller and more reluctant to take market risks.

Even in successful private ventures, the collaboration and partnership could often be undermined by the conflict of individual interests. There were cases in which brothers had disputes over properties they invested in together, and sisters-in-law quarreled and fought each other in order to claim a bigger share. In cases of interest conflicts within extended families, it became a norm to prioritize one's immediate family as opposed to the extended family. As such, the highlighted interests of small families not only raised issues for relative contributions and gains from migrant work between siblings in an extended family, as discussed in the previous section, but also led to disputes in private businesses. Although the brotherhood relations were important in pooling and mobilizing the limited resources in the village, it was difficult to maintain and extend the businesses to a larger scale. Unlike the unitary household model, peasants adapted their strategies to bargain for more individualistic interests within the household, and businesses based on kinship or lineage networks were vulnerable to both market risks and lack of trust between partners.

Family cooperation and individual pursuits

Most married couples in Han Village adopted the patrilocal residential pattern; daughters were expected to marry out and brides might come from a neighboring village or township, or from another province. In the sample, around 24 percent of the wives married from the same village, 57 percent married from nearby villages (within the same county), 12 percent married from other areas within the province, and 8 percent married from other provinces. People have been marrying across the local major ethnic groups, most commonly the Han–Manchu intermarriages.

Traditionally, most women married into the husbands' family and relied on the husband to earn incomes to fund housing construction and life events. Their work patterns were thus expected to comply with the "virtues" of being good daughters-in-law and wives. Lianying, a 45-year-old woman when interviewed in 2007, recalled a family conflict when she just married into the family in 1985 at the age of 23. She felt very sick one day and could not go to the family farm; this was seen by her in-laws as failing to perform as a virtuous daughter-in-law:

> In fact I was pregnant and that's why I felt sick, but I didn't know that. I should have worked in the field to farm with my in-laws, but on that day I just stayed at home and did some light domestic work. My in-laws told my husband. I was beaten by him. This was the only time that he has ever used violence toward me. He was nice to me in fact, and I did not resent him. I know it was because of my in-laws.

Lianying was beaten by her husband because it was considered unacceptable that "a lazy daughter-in-law would rest at home, leaving old people to farm alone" at that time. Although it was not clear what her in-laws told her husband, Lianying was clearly perceived to be the one to be disciplined to comply with the "virtues" of being obedient and hardworking in the fields. But over time, such virtues lost significance. A study in Shaanxi villages suggested a similar case of family conflict, and when the daughter-in-law refused to go to the field, other family members had to give in and compromise (Greenhalgh & Li, 1995).

The legends of "old virtues" were still told occasionally for fun among villagers, and it was said that the previous expectation of daughters-in-law to be obedient to their mothers-in-law was particularly important in Manchu families. Daughters-in-law had to "pay respect to the mother-in-law in the morning, serve meals in their rooms and clean up afterward."[16] Nowadays in both Manchu and Han ethnic groups, old women no longer enjoy such authority, and mothers-in-law said that they did not mind preparing meals for young women if they were busy "earning money." Young women gained more say when economic resources were less coordinated in an extended family but more determined by individualized work in the market. In the studies of other villages in China, it was often related with the rise of "girl power" due to the emerging earning opportunities for young people (Yan, 2006). In Han Village, such a change was more related with the fact that the extended family had little resources to provide, and young people often had to seek individual earning opportunities outside home.

Over time, the conjugal bonds gained more importance in both economic and emotional terms. When Lianying told her story of being beaten by her husband in a version that emphasized "a pregnant woman being beaten by the husband due to the gossip of the in-laws," most of the blame was on her in-laws. The intergenerational relationship was posited as the damaging force, rather than the coordinating force within the extended family, and Lianying used this as the reason to forgive her husband with her focus on the conjugal relationship for which she felt satisfied in general.

Along with the changing expectation of a "proper" wife and daughter-in-law, the self-realization of women gained more importance compared with the hardworking ethics and multitasking practices. In early reform years, the farming tasks were yet to be mechanized, and some middle-aged women recalled being exhausted in farming and domestic work. These tasks became "lighter" or less important over time, as people minimized their labor investment in farming, grew trees on farms, and expected little income from raising livestock or running sidelines. Women faced more diverse work options outside home, and their relations with parents or in-laws also changed accordingly.

A new trend was that parents provided help in farming and domestic work for their children, so that young men and women could take up migrant work or explore other market opportunities. For example, a mother-in-law had taken care of the farm for several years because her daughter-in-law worked as a waitress in her brother's small restaurant in the nearby county. But such a pattern was contingent on family structures. If the woman married an elder brother and had an early family split, the husband might not need to contribute his wage income to the extended family anymore, while the wife might need to be earthbound and stay at home. If a woman was married to the youngest brother and lived with in-laws afterward, she might get help in family responsibilities and farm work from in-laws and could pursue other work opportunities.[17] Theoretically, as farm work became easier to manage, old people could free young people to work outside home for longer times. But in reality, because old couples usually had multiple adult children and only worked closely with one of the couples, many young women still stayed at home when such help was not available.

Along with the changing intergenerational relationship, the patrilineal and patrilocal family structure remained dominant: parents helped to construct housing for their son to get married, and the son inherited the land and property and provided the elderly support to his parents. More importantly, the housing residential plot was still adjusted largely based on the number of sons in the village. But over time, many families had begun to adopt more flexible relations with sons and daughters and the corresponding resource flows were more diversified.

This was partly related with changes in reproduction behaviors. People still generally wanted to have a son, but if the family had several sons, it became too burdensome to repeat housing construction for each of them, and there might be disputes about the division of property and care work. As such, some respondents felt that "one son is enough,"[18] and some others only wished to have a daughter after they had a son. Although Han Village had a loose family planning policy that had allowed each woman to have two children, "thanks to the high concentration of ethnic minorities,"[19] the fertility rate had declined over time. Given the escalating costs of living expenses, schooling, marriage, and housing construction, the average number of children decreased from 4.5 to 1 over generations in the sample (Table 5.3). Around half of middle-aged respondents had two children, and more young people chose to have only one child.

The declining number of children made it possible for more family resources to be directed toward daughters, and the relationship between women and their natal families became more flexible to deal with difficulties that young women and their parents might face in their own lives. Women who married from the same village or neighboring villages often maintained frequent interactions with their natal families, which involved mutual economic and emotional support as

Table 5.3 Number of children in the sample in Han Village

Mother born in	1		2		3		4		5 and more		Total	Average
1930s					25%				75%		4	4.5
1940s			13%		50%		13%		25%		8	3.5
1950s	11%		40%		37%		6%		6%		19	2.6
1960s	39%		50%		11%						18	1.7
1970s	46%		54%								13	1.5
1980s	100%										2	1
Total	17	27%	25	39%	14	22%	2	3%	6	9%	64	

Note: The number of children is missing for one out of 65 cases, so there are 64 valid cases. If the mother's age is missing, the father's age is used as an approximate. The blank cells are used to refer to 0%.

well as help in care work. In Yue's case, she received economic resources from her natal family in running a retail store. As the only daughter, she remained in close contact with her parents, and this created some room for her entrepreneurship in the male-dominated businesses.

Although many men would give their wages to their wives when they returned from their migrant work, women still wanted to have the ability to earn their own money, ranging from running a shop to taking home-based or part-time jobs. The desire was seen as acceptable by in-laws that young women wanted to "spend their own money and need not to explain to anyone,"[20] and in-laws would not take it as offending. When the source of income was increasingly derived from individuals rather than from the family farms, women's earning activities were tolerated to a greater extent.

Meanwhile, some women still chose to be stay-at-home mothers, but those who returned to the village from their migrant work were relatively inexperienced in agricultural tasks[21] and were less willing to go to the fields. Many planned to resume work after a while, by returning to the paid labor force, running a small shop, or joining the family business. Some of the options did not require a separation from their children. As such, behind the increasing "girl power" (Yan, 2006) lay the new forms of tied migration or working intermittently to avoid family separation or to serve the rising significance of motherhood (Evans, 2010).

Urban dream and rural base

With limited local entrepreneurial dynamics, villagers faced stiffer market competition in the labor market and their businesses were threatened by external capital. Not only did the local quarry owners give up their businesses to external competitors, but also the ordinary peasant households began to rent their land as storage sites for quarries at a price of 300 yuan per mu every year, and such private transactions were tolerated by village cadres.[22] Even for peasants who had complained about the noise and dust that were generated by quarries, the village leadership left it to be solved by private negotiations between two parties, and the families whose homes were affected received compensation directly from the quarry owners. When cadres were asked about the noises and pollution generated by quarries, their reaction was "the provision of the permit was regulated by the state," or "the transaction and compensation was between private parties, and the village office did not play a role."[23]

As such, the village was no longer the place in which villagers shared and defended their common interests as a community. Some had hoped the village leadership would "regulate" the quarry businesses in the name of public well-being, but the village leadership was reluctant to intervene in "private" businesses except collecting rents and procedural fees. Instead, cadres tended to use some material benefits that entrepreneurs contributed to the community to justify their business operations based on the "market efficiency" logic. Villagers recalled that once each family received a bottle of oil, a package of rice, and other food from a private boss. However, some respondents felt that such a "lobbying" strategy did not always work, and they pointed out that such benefits were "too small" to result in gratitude when the private bosses took over quarries but did not hire many locals.[24] Such a recruiting practice was rational for employers, because migrant workers from outside were more "disciplined and easy to control" and did not have a lot of "local affairs" to take care of.[25]

Unlike the morally enveloped community described by Scott (1976), cadres had set their new goal as not to be the obstacle of villagers to make their own decisions either to outsource their land or to get compensation, since they had little collective resources to offer. This was closely related with the central government's shift to non-coercive and "harmonious" approaches, as well as the logic of market efficiency. To serve social harmony, the village leadership had focused more on avoiding conflicts with villagers. To serve market efficiency, private transactions and compensation between enterprises and villagers were allowed and tolerated by the village office to maximize the utility of the affected villagers and their families.

The disintegrated community and the lack of local economic opportunities had pushed peasants from land to pursue their urban dream mainly through migrant work. To seek better opportunities elsewhere, young people like Haitao quit school and started migrant work at an early age. However, their further career development was hindered by their limited qualifications, and Haitao was depressed to find that he could never earn a wage of white-collar workers. In Han Village, education level had increased over generations, but Haitao saw a "glass ceiling" for rural children to become quality labor. To some extent, their education opportunities were adversely affected by market reforms, partly due to the concentration of education resources in "good schools" in urban and town centers that Haitao's family could not afford to send him to. For rural parents, it was a difficult choice whether to pursue costly education in good schools for an unrealistic urban dream, or to follow the practical plan to make immediate income.

The greater awareness of the importance of "quality labor" made respondents more prepared to send their children to receive higher education than themselves. Although respondents mostly had middle school and at most high school educations, which was considered "enough" in migrant work, they in general had higher expectations for their children. It was illustrated by the comparison between the highest education levels within the couples in the sample and that of their children. For couples, 24 percent had primary school education, 45 percent went to middle school, 22 percent went to high school, and 0 percent went to universities; but for their children's highest education, 2 percent had primary school education, 10 percent went to middle school, 24 percent went to high school, and 28 percent went to universities, in addition to 36 percent who were still attending schools.

Education seemed to provide the most gender-neutral opportunities to realize urban dreams, particularly for the economically better-off families. Among other mechanisms leading toward the urban dream, young men could join the military service as a stepping stone toward urban jobs, and marriage migration was more likely to be a feasible vehicle for young women. Young people who had failed in their own urban dream also embraced the urban ideal of education more readily for their children, partly due to their recent migration and exposure to city life. Young parents like Juhai seemed to project their urban dream onto their precious children and wanted "the best" for them.

But in Han Village, the urban dream of young people was closely linked with their close relationship with parents or in-laws. The young couple of Juhai was able to do migrant work because they could rely on the grandparents for farming and child caring. Although they tried to raise their daughter with an urban lifestyle, the little girl was left behind in the village with her grandparents when the parents left for migrant work. The urban commercial culture helped to create an illusionary urban dream, which was ironically closely related with their attachment to the rural base, the thrifty life led by grandparents, and the separation of parents and children. Such an urban dream was very real for young people who grew up under the wide TV and Internet coverage in the village. They embraced urban consumerism and believed that Beijing was just several hours away.

However, Beijing was more than "several hours away." Given the large scales of labor influx into the lower tiers of the labor market, their migrant jobs were unstable and subject to the need of the urban economy. There were several occasions when migrant workers were "cleaned away" from Beijing for the "image of the city." Around the time of the Olympic Games, many construction sites were closed and migrant workers went back home. In many cases, migrant workers had to return home for market fluctuations or policy changes. For them, the urban dream was both close and far away: the allure of urban life was nearby but settling down in the cities was difficult.

Haitao was one year younger than Juhai, but he had moved away from migrant work and turned to private businesses, which was the ultimate goal for many migrant workers who saved money and returned from cities with a failed urban dream. If there were better opportunities to work for themselves, migrant work was in fact the "second-best" option for peasants in many cases (Guang & Zheng, 2005). In a place of limited economic resources for ordinary villagers, Haitao's market adventure was greatly facilitated by his good connections, including that of his sworn brothers and male relatives and friends. Although villagers turned to the male kin networks or the sworn brotherhood to facilitate economic cooperation activities, the conflicts of self-interests had made the "male-bonding" relationships vulnerable, as the traditional moral basis of "trust" was often overridden by market rationality. The market penetration and the expansion of urban capital had further undermined the competitiveness of local businesses.

In Han Village, having a rural base remained important because of the peasants' access to residential plots and self-built housing. Peasants were more able to utilize their social networks in the village, to enjoy the support among family members, and to just consume home-grown vegetables. But on the other hand, the underdevelopment of local industries and businesses in the face of urban capital still highlighted the urban-rural boundary in the job hierarchy. Furthermore, Han Village was not a peaceful countryside for rural nostalgia but was another site of stratification. Better-off families could afford to build well-designed, good-quality housing in separate yards for each son, while poor families could only afford to extend the existing construction with no decorations. Some tried to help their children to escape rural poverty, and others saw a hope of forming partnerships in rural businesses. Such differentiation was also closely related with the resource and emotional relations in the gender and family dynamics, which was often ignored by class analyses.

At the household level, the rise of migrant work seemed to suggest the process of "individualization" (Yan, 2009) and the celebration of "girl power," but it also illustrated the importance of "householding" (Jacka, 2012) in China's countryside. Despite the individualization of earning opportunities in migrant work, the "brotherhood" relationship and family cooperation had been important in "men's businesses" of quarries and transportation given the limited local business opportunities, which diverged from "women's businesses" of stores and barbershops, sometimes inherited from women's natal families. Meanwhile, the "householding" processes had diversified to allow some young women to be mobile migrant workers by leaving children to grandparents and moving together with their husbands. The mixed trends of individualization, "householding," and "male bonding" were embedded in the understanding of the rising opportunities in the market and the limited resources within the community. Although people hoped to escape rurality and embrace urban modernity, they had to rely on different channels of pooling and mobilizing resources that were embedded in their rural base, and many still wanted to have a fallback option if their urban dream failed.

Notes

1 Ying County Archive Committee (Ying County difangzhi bianzuanweiyuanhui). 1999. *Ying County Archive* (Ying County zhi). Beijing: Central Compilation & Translation Press (Zhongyang bianyi chubanshe), p. 198.
2 Ying County Archive, p. 204.
3 Interview with Juzhi, Wenchang, 2007.
4 Interview with Juzhi, 2008, 2010.
5 Hebei Provincial Government (Hebei sheng renmin zhengfu). 2012. *Hebei Yearbook (Hebei nianjian)*. Hebei: Hebei Yearbook Publisher (Hebei nianjianchubanshe), p. 53.
6 The Central Committee of the Chinese Communist Party set the lease for 15 years and then extended it to 30 years. See Law of the People's Republic of China on the Contracting of Rural Land, effective from 2003.
7 Ying County Archive, pp. 441–444.
8 Interview with village cadres, 2008.
9 Interview with Juzhi, 2009.
10 In ideal cases, 1 mu of corn can have an annual yield of 500 kilograms and 1 mu of wheat can have an annual yield of 400 kilograms, but for many families, the harvest usually reached 70 to 80 percent of that of the best years due to the limited rainfall.
11 Interview with Wenyu, 2009.
12 Interview with Shulin, 2010.
13 Interview with Wujie, 2011.
14 Interview with Wencai and his wife, 2010.

15 Interview with Juzhi, 2010.
16 Interview with Shuqing, 2007; Lianying, 2007.
17 But depending on how capable and willing to help grandparents are, living in the
    extended families also suggests another possibility that young women may have
    more housework to do, which was the case for some other families in the sample.
18 Interview with Xuemin, 2007.
19 Interview with Aiti, 2007; Jujing, 2007.
20 Interview with Wenzen, 2008.
21 Similar finding was noticed by Jacka (2012).
22 Interview with Juzhi, 2009.
23 Interview with village cadres, 2009.
24 Interview with Shulin, 2010.
25 Interview with Juzhi, 2009.

References

Evans, H. (2010). The gender of communication: Changing expectations of mothers
  and daughters in urban China. *The China Quarterly, 204*, 980–1000.
Greenhalgh, S., & Li, J. (1995). Engendering reproductive policy and practice in
  peasant China: For a feminist demography of reproduction. *Signs, 20*, 601–641.
Guang, L., & Zheng, L. (2005). Migration as the second-best option: Local power
  and off-farm employment. *The China Quarterly, 181*, 22–45.
Jacka, T. (2012). Migration, householding and the well-being of left-behind women
  in rural Ningxia. *The China Journal, 67*, 1–21.
Judd, E. R. (2002). *The Chinese women's movement between state and market*. Stan-
  ford, CA: Stanford University Press.
Scott, J. (1976). *The moral economy of the peasant*. New Haven, CT: Yale University
  Press.
Yan, Y. (2006). Girl power: Young women and the waning of patriarchy in rural north
  China. *Ethnology, 45*(2), 105–124.
Yan, Y. (2009). *The individualization of Chinese society*. Oxford and New York: Berg.

6 Ning Village

Integrated or marginalized in urbanization

Ning Village is located near the municipality of Yinchuan, the provincial capital of Ningxia Ethnic Autonomous Region. The municipality governs three urban districts, two counties, and a county-level city. In administrative terms, Ning Village belongs to one of the urban districts of the municipality, but it is located on the edge of the urban district and is close to the rural areas of a neighboring county. Before land development, the village used to belong to Spring Township, and the township was urbanized and the township office was replaced by a street office, with only a distance of 2.5 kilometers from the municipality center.

Ning Village had been a typical inland rural community economically reliant on farming, with a mix of outmigration and local petty businesses, and it had been among the best irrigated areas in the region. The main crops had been wheat, grain, and corn. In 2000, Ning Village was combined with a neighboring village into one big administrative village. The other village used to belong to the neighboring county and was taken into the administration of the expanding urban district. But the two natural villages were geographically separated by a river and remained relatively independent of each other in grassroots economic activities. The urbanization process occurred in Ning Village first and then was extended to the neighboring village, and the relocation processes were carried out separately with different resettlement neighborhoods. As such, this chapter concentrates on the original Ning Village before the merge.

Before land development, Ning Village had around 524 households and a population of around 3,826, which was divided into 10 villagers' groups (or teams). Due to the proximity of the village to the urban center of Yinchuan, some villagers, mostly men and young women, had been engaged in some migrant work. Other than that, some families raised livestock or grew vegetables for the urban markets, and some ran small businesses like food processing, but there were no sizable local industries before land development. Located between the urban center and the rural county, the village also had some businesses for taxi drivers and transportation. The annual income per capita was around 3,100 yuan in 2003,[1] with a combination of farming, migrant work, and petty businesses. This was close to the average for rural residents of the whole municipality of Yinchuan, which was 2,961 yuan in 2002,[2] and higher than that of the whole province (1,917 yuan for rural residents in 2002).[3] At that time, the peasants in the suburban area of Yinchuan reached a level of 3,407 yuan (including Ning Village),[4] which was possibly due to the compensation villagers received from land expropriation. Along with urbanization, the annual income per capita had increased to 4,917 yuan for the Yinchuan area in 2008.[5]

Although lagging behind in economy development in the early reform years, local governments became actively involved in the land development projects as a tool to catch up with the early developed coastal areas. In the 1990s, Ning Village had witnessed incremental land development. Under the new national strategy to develop the West that was initiated in 2000, the municipality further expanded its development plan to construct the "Greater Yinchuan" around 2002. Before land development, the village used to have around 4,000 mu of arable land, which decreased to 3,000 mu in 2002[6] and was mostly expropriated by 2008. There had been limited resistance against the government-sponsored development projects, but villagers had learned to negotiate for more compensation. When the land development projects were expanded from one team to another, compensation prices had increased over time. The land development led to a one-off compensation for the land, and peasants' employment transition occurred in a short period of time. As such, the great driving force behind people's employment patterns was not rural industries but urbanization and zoning by governments and developers.

Field visits to Ning Village were carried out in 2001, 2002, 2003, 2005, 2006, 2007, 2009, and 2010. This chapter drew on in-depth interviews with 54 couples: for 16 of them, only the husband was interviewed; for 18 of them, only the wife was interviewed; for 20 of them, both the husband and the wife were interviewed (a daughter was also interviewed in one case in this group). In total, there were 75 respondents (36 men and 39 women). The age of the wife ranged from 25 to 76 at the time of the investigation, and the age of the husband ranged from 24 to 74. Five of them were cadres in the village and villagers' teams.

Losing land and leaving farming?

Ning Village is located in an area where the water supply for farms is less constrained by rainfall compared with other inland areas, benefiting from the Yellow River that runs across the Yinchuan municipality. The area also had relatively large amounts of land. When collective land was redistributed to individual households in 1982, each eligible peasant was assigned an amount of 2–2.5 mu of land, depending on the teams they belonged to. Peasants had tried growing various crops in addition to the traditional categories of wheat and corn, including beans, grain, peanuts, and so on. Many villagers used to grow wheat or corn in the first half of the year, and grain for the second half of the year, but more and more villagers withdrew from the intense crop cycles. To some extent, agricultural productivity was constrained by the increasing costs of inputs and the low prices of agricultural products, as Jacka (2012) found in her fieldwork in Ningxia. Many villagers said that the local agricultural production could meet the self-sufficient level, but they "could not make a lot of profit out of it." With the limited profit room from farming, peasants had tried to explore other agriculture-related opportunities, such as growing vegetables and transporting them to the urban markets. This had been an important source of cash income for some families.

Due to the lack of local industries, villagers had relied on family sideline activities and migration for income in addition to farming. But unlike other inland areas where the more capable peasants needed to travel long distance to get migrant work, villagers in Ning Village were more tied to their rural base. Due to its proximity with the urban center, villagers could take advantage of the market demand as petty commodity producers. Some of the family sideline businesses, such as livestock raising and food processing, were extensions of their agricultural production, and such a combination allowed accommodating more family labor in petty household production.

As such, farming became the foundation of other income-generating activities and still involved some capable workers rather than being left to less firm laborers as part of the "inside" work. But in general, women were more active in both farming and sideline businesses, particularly middle-aged groups. For the cohort born in the 1950s in the sample, the proportion of major laborers in farming was 20 percent for men and 50 percent for women in the 1990s, while that of sideline businesses was 25 percent for men and 31 percent for women. Similar gender gaps remained for other cohorts as well. Compared with farming, the gender gap was smaller for sideline activities, and in some cases, men were even more represented in running sideline activities in the recent two decades. It occurred in some rural areas that men took over the specialized household business previously run by women when it became more attractive (Jacka, 1997), but in Ning Village, the more common situation was that some men joined these sideline activities after they quit migrant jobs or did not have better employment opportunities. Some had been too old to do other jobs or escaped from harsh working conditions of migrant work, and others used sideline work as a transitional job while staying at home before finding a better one. In general, women concentrated on their sideline activities longer and took them more seriously than men did, but over time, both men and women tended to reduce their involvement in both farming and sideline activities due to land development.

With the expansion of land development projects, some peasants complained that the land quality and farming conditions had been deteriorating. With more land being taken away, the irrigation network of water flows was cut and reconstructed, which had negative impacts on the irrigation of other land that was yet to be developed. "We could not grow crops like before, even if the land were still there: there was no water (coming) into the land."[7] However, villagers also found it important to continue and intensify farming, because land compensation would be calculated based on the amount of land as well as crops in the land. Some villagers even grew fruit trees in their fields, and in land development, each tree was compensated with a handsome price of several hundred yuan.

The land development and compensation processes were still subject to the implementation of policies that varied across teams. In this process, villagers' teams played a more important role, because land distribution and adjustment had been largely managed at the team level.[8] For teams that were developed at different time periods, the "compensation price" in 1995 was 8,000 yuan per mu, 10,000 yuan in 1998, and around 30,000 yuan in 2003. The increase of land price reflected the changing expectation of villagers. As such, the process of urbanization fueled the enthusiasm of villagers to cherish their land. Many villagers illustrated the dispossessed feeling and a desire to hold on to their land. Their landholding position was to some extent transformed into their bargaining power, and the expectation of their land to be exchanged for a better price had continued to increase over time throughout the development process.

As such, peasants' attachment to land revived to make sure it would be trans-lated into other economic resources. In one of the teams that had vast amount of land to be developed, some villagers effectively mobilized collective wills to bargain with governments. Because this team's land would be used to build the main relocation housing neighborhoods, the newly elected team leadership sug-gested that the team should have the right to keep a small piece of land, and the team would use the collective land compensation to build a single-family housing neighborhood for team members. The proposal was agreed to by local govern-ments in exchange for the team's cooperation in the development process. As a result, land was converted into not only monetary compensation but also hous-ing properties. Prior to land development, a few villagers who "luckily" got urban jobs or migrated to other places had given up their land to others. Now these vil-lagers regretted that they had missed a golden opportunity to gain a share in the redistribution of economic resources according to one's landholding position. At the moment of rural-to-urban transition, the land-cherishing mood reflected the desire of villagers to catch the last chance to exert their advantage as "insiders."

Distant or transplanted employment opportunities

Laosun, a 52-year-old man when interviewed in 2002, had been a brigade leader in the Maoist era. He had two sons and three daughters, and when the farms were redistributed to households in 1982, the family got 16 mu of land for eight family members (including his mother, who lived with them). With a large amount of land to farm, he soon quit the position of the brigade leader. With five children and a parent to support, Laosun and his wife were in great need of income and felt it was difficult to catch up with other villagers who had begun to rebuild their homes in the 1980s. The couple started growing vegetables and traded vegeta-bles between the village and the urban market. However, the more pressing need to build new houses and marry their children urged Laosun to find other ways to make cash income, and he joined other villagers as a migrant worker. He recalled:

> People began to rebuild their homes after the land was redistributed. It was not enough to rely on money from the land, and many people started

going out to work from the 1980s. But our kids were small at that time, and we had a large amount of land to farm. Because it was a suburban area, we had advantages. We grew vegetables, and carried our vegetables to the city using bicycles. We did not have much manpower; otherwise we could have built greenhouses for vegetables. Children grew up and my eldest son took 6 mu of land. It was in the 1990s, and I went to Yinchuan to work in a construction project. I followed a local boss and did some management work for him. My wife still grew vegetables at home. It was necessary to have someone on both sides, as we needed money from both sides, and vegetables alone could make several hundred yuan per mu in a year. . . . We built a new house in 1997, because we promised our daughter-in-law when she married in that we would build the house in the next year (of the marriage).

As such, migration was often timed by both social changes and family life cycles. For Laosun, his migrant work was a short life episode to finance housing construction and to marry off his sons. Otherwise, people would rather find some local work instead. The proportion of migrant work had increased steadily under the market reform relative to that of local work until the 1990s, and then dropped to zero in the 2000s after the area was urbanized. Even when migrant work had been a popular choice in the 1980s, it was not a necessary choice for many who were satisfied with their lives as "petty commodity producers," as described by Gates (1996). After periods of short-term migration, many families turned to locally based sideline businesses, which allowed them to keep their farms cultivated and involved close cooperation among family members. In addition to running stands in the nearby urban areas to sell agricultural products, peasant families had been involved in various sideline businesses, including raising livestock, making rice noodles, driving a taxi, and so on, to make the most out of the local economic opportunities.

However, some respondents commented that their petty production was often constrained by market saturation. Given the limited family accumulations and market uncertainties, many families continued to rely on both petty production and migrant work. Gender differences remained in that men dominated both local and migrant work; women were less likely to take the jobs as individuals and tended to multitask in farming and sideline activities at home. The only two exceptions in Table 6.1 where women were more represented than men in local or migrant work were due to the existence of two cases of migrant women among a small number of women in the cohorts. One old woman was divorced and had to work as a security guard in a state-owned enterprise, and the other was a young woman who worked as a restaurant waitress in a neighboring county for several years. In general, women were rooted in the family economy and less visible in Table 6.1 until the 2000s. But prior to land development, many men put their jobs on hold and returned to "watch" land and construct housing.

Still, land development projects had given some hope to villagers by generating more job opportunities and shifting the urban-rural boundary. For most cohorts

Table 6.1 Local and migrant wage workers in the sample in Ning Village

Born in	Gender	Number	1950s L	1950s M	1960s L	1960s M	1970s L	1970s M	1980s L	1980s M	1990s L	1990s M	2000s L	2000s M
1930s	M	2	100%		50%		50%							
	F	1												
1940s	M	6			33%	17%	17%	17%	33%	17%	33%		66%	
	F	4										25%¹		25%¹
1950s	M	20	/	/	5%	5%	35%	10%	45%	10%	25%	10%	40%	5%
	F	16	/	/			6%						19%	
1960s	M	9	/	/	/	/		11%	11%	22%	11%	22%	33%	
	F	6	/	/	/	/							33%	
1970s	M	8	/	/	/	/	/	/	/	/	17%	13%	50%	13%
	F	6	/	/	/	/	/	/	/	/			17%	
1980s	M	1	/	/	/	/	/	/	/	/	/	/		
	F	1	/	/	/	/	/	/	/	/	/	/		100%²
Not Clear	M	2											50%	
	F	1												
Total		83												

L = local workers, M = migrant workers.

Note: Among 54 couples, there were 48 men and 35 women (83 in total) who had complete working trajectory information. "/" means "not applicable" and the blank cells are used to refer to 0%.

[1] This percent indicates an exceptional case of one woman who worked outside the village: she was divorced and worked as a security guard for an urban work unit for seven years to support herself and her children.

[2] This percent indicates an exceptional case of one woman who worked outside the village: she worked as a waitress in a restaurant in the neighboring county for several years.

in the sample (born in the 1940s–1970s), the proportions of having a local job were higher in the 2000s than in previous decades for both men and women, ranging from 17 percent to 66 percent. This reversed the previous trend that some middle-aged men put their jobs on hold due to land development. The proportion of men born in the 1950s who had local jobs increased from 25 percent in the 1990s to 40 percent in the 2000s; for their female counterparts, it increased from 0 percent in the 1990s to 19 percent in the 2000s. However, the proportion of being migrant workers decreased to zero for all cohorts, which suggested that people did not need to migrate over a distance to find a job.

Urbanization, however, increased the expectation of villagers about job search. But villagers soon realized that it was not easy to get good jobs in the center of the municipality, and many respondents suggested that these jobs were not for them. In their eyes, the corporations and companies established in the new industrial or commercial centers were not really "local," but were "transplanted" and had no responsibility to take care of locals. Most transplanted employers had selective recruitment processes and were driven by profit-seeking incentives. "Only young and educated" people could get "white-collar jobs in these buildings," according to many respondents. This contributed to a limited increase level of employment (local and migrant) in the 2000s than in the previous decades (from 16 percent in the 1990s to 31 percent in the 2000s) in the sample. Although the proportion holding local jobs increased, this took place together with the decrease in migrant jobs, and many people were unwilling to work under harsh conditions with the new compensation and properties at hand.

With more people turning from migrant jobs to local jobs after land development, the gender gap remained but was closed particularly in the middle-aged cohorts. In the 2000s, the gender difference in the proportions holding local employment was 40 percent to 19 percent for those born in the 1950s in the sample; 33 percent to 33 percent for those born in the 1960s; and 50 percent to 17 percent for those born in the 1970s. Women in their 40s and 50s witnessed a sharper rise in the chance of having local jobs in the 2000s not only compared with younger women, but also compared with their male counterparts. Among these middle-aged women, the most common jobs were to clean the floors in the commercial centers, collect trash in the buildings, and cook for the construction sites. Although men still outnumbered women with regard to employment, it was largely due to the continuing gender inequality in employment structures rather than a response to new economic opportunities. In 2000, among eight men who had local jobs in the cohort born in the 1950s in the sample, five had held employment before land development, such as village cadres and organization staff. Most of them continued with their previous work or found new jobs based on their previous networks, whereas the increase in women's local jobs reflected more of the demand of the expanding urban economy. Their adaptive employment choices helped to draw them out of the domestic sphere, but their jobs were still concentrated in the low-end labor market.

Women's flexibility was related with their role in the long-standing family cooperation patterns. In the rural household economy, women often received limited social recognition for their economic contribution, and they felt it easier to take up less prestigious jobs. Some women were in fact long to become urban residents and take individualized work, because of the heavy burden of multi-tasking in the family economy and living the village life. Yueqing, a 35-year-old woman when interviewed in 2010, had felt her life to be too tiring before land development. When Yueqing got married in 1996, she quit her job as an elementary school teacher with an expectation that "the husband would be in charge of the outside and the wife would take care of the inside." Yueqing's husband worked as a migrant worker only for a short time and returned due to health problems. The family thus relied heavily on Yueqing to farm and raise pigs. Even with the help of her husband and in-laws, Yueqing felt depressed and tried to find a way to escape. At that time, the village had been gradually urbanized and the village council wanted to recruit some "educated and capable" female staff. At the beginning, her in-laws were not very happy for Yueqing's endeavor to go to the public sphere, but Yueqing was confident that she could balance family and work quite well.

> The recruitment, here was my chance. It is not a job that you need to be in the office nine to five, you can finish it at home. I would not apply for a job that required too much service. I didn't have that much energy. But this job, I could take care of family and work at the same time. My husband was very supportive as well. Just to distribute pamphlets and ask women to register for all kinds of things.

Yueqing was recruited into the village council largely because of her middle school education and teaching experience, and was soon appointed as the new women's officer of the village. As one of the few young and educated female cadres, she was soon selected to be a candidate of the community officer for one of the new residential neighborhoods. Such salaried positions needed to be filled by someone with local knowledge and networks, and an appropriate level of education. Yueqing fit these criteria well, and she was happy that she did not need to farm and raise pigs anymore. Yueqing's husband, who used to be too weak to be a capable farmer, also became a salaried worker in an entertainment center in the nearby commercial center. In this process, the family turned from a household-level cooperation pattern in farming and livestock raising to the pursuit of independent careers.

For such an employment transition, the most "prepared" group in urbanization were those who were young and educated. The transition could benefit families like Yueqing's, whose manpower to farm and raise pigs was limited but had some human capital and work experiences to fit in urban wage sectors. In addition to individualized work, families like Yueqing's conducted other businesses based on their land compensation and housing properties, such as transportation and rental business. The following section discusses such business opportunities, given the property boom accompanied by urbanization.

Property boom and businesses in the urbanization process

Yukui, a 46-year-old man when interviewed in 2006, had been working as a migrant at construction sites since the age of 20 for around 20 years, but he spent only several months every year as a migrant worker outside of the village. At the same time, his wife had stayed in the village to farm 5 mu of the family farm and took care of two daughters. Since 1999, Yukui stayed at home longer to build more housing constructions in the family. In 1999, he spent 20,000 yuan to build three rooms of self-built house as a new home for the family. Around the same time, villagers began to intensify housing construction and used their extra rooms in self-built housing to generate rental income. Similar to Yukui, many migrant workers returned home to build houses. The intensification of constructions reached a peak during 1999–2003, when large-scale land development was going on. In 2003, the villagers' team that Yukui belonged to had around 400 team members, but also accommodated about 1600 outsiders who rented housing from villagers and did migrant work in the nearby city center.

As house construction became the most important "job" at the end of the 1990s and the beginning of the 2000s, Yukui joined to build more housing in 2002. He spent 70,000 yuan on constructing 400 square meters of housing for residence and commercial use, including six residential rooms and one shopfront room (*menmianfang*). To do that, he borrowed 60,000 yuan from the local economic cooperative. The cost for housing construction mostly ranged from 20,000 to 100,000 yuan, and the constructed floor space in general ranged from 100 to 400 square meters. The housing cost for self-built housing was between 200 and 500 yuan per square meter. But such dense construction on the same housing plot was often regarded as illegal when the villagers did not get official permission. Official prohibitive measures had been weak, but when more and more villagers invested in the intensification of self-built housing, the municipal and district governments initiated crackdown movements in the early 2000s. Team cadres had to negotiate with local governments to defend the villagers' "indigenous" interests, and in some cases, villagers agreed to stop their illegal construction, in exchange for the governments' tolerance so that their current self-built housing would not be torn down.

Such self-built housing helped to generate rental incomes for villagers. Yukui's family earned a rent of 7,000 yuan from the shopfront room, and another rent of 3,000 yuan from the other six rooms in a year. Similar to Yukui, many villagers put their work on hold to invest more in properties and wait for rents and future compensation. However, the returns of housing investments were often too slow to help peasants to pay back the loans and debts that were borrowed to finance housing construction. As such, rental incomes needed to be supplemented by other sources of income. Among the 17 respondents' families who had run rental business (47 percent of the 36 families who ever ran private businesses), only 3 of them were only doing rental business, and others were multitasking in other businesses, including transportation (14, 39 percent) and commercial business (11, 31 percent). The cases that had switched between multiple businesses accounted for 53 percent of the interviewed families who had conducted businesses (19 out of 36).

Before land development, such multitasking had been common for agriculture-related businesses. In addition to farming, 12 of the 54 interviewed families had been engaged in running vegetable stands or processing agricultural products, and 8 specialized in livestock raising. The typical gender division of labor at that time was that men moved back and forth between migrant work and local work, and women were more active in taking care of family sidelines. However, these agriculture-related businesses declined with land development because it was not feasible and compatible with the urban living space.

There still remained 11 small commercial businesses run by respondents, including retail stores, public baths, and trade business. Among the 11 businesses, 3 were established in the 1970s, 1 in the 1980s, 2 in the 1990s, and 5 in the 2000s. After land development, both men and women witnessed an increase in the proportion of being involved in such businesses. For example, a young woman had returned from her migrant work to sell small accessories by renting a counter in a newly developed commercial center, where she met her future husband, who was doing similar business, and they combined and expanded their business after marriage. Table 6.2 suggests that this category had somewhat increased for young people from the 1990s to the 2000s. In the 2000s, middle-aged men (born in the 1950s and the 1960s) seemed to be more active than their female counterparts, but for the cohort in their 30s (born in the 1970s), women were more represented in such businesses. A few stores were run by couples, and it created more room for women to adopt flexible working schedules to balance work and family.

Yukui's family also adopted a diversification strategy that took advantage of various sources of income. In 2002, part of the family's land was taken away, and Yukui's wife only needed to farm the remaining 3 mu of land. She began to commute to an urban work unit as a temporary janitor. Yukui also quit migrant work due to his growing age and worsened health, and began to run a retail store in his own house around 2003. However, the store did not generate a reliable income. To enhance their economic security, the family continued to expand their investment in housing, including buying a single-family house in 2003 at an insider's price of 60,000 yuan. For this purpose, the family borrowed another 70,000 yuan. It was common among villagers that their ambitious plans to be "landlords" led to heavy financial burdens and resulted in difficult choices. Yukui's family had to sell the single-family house at a price of 250,000 yuan. After paying off debts, the family still had 100,000 yuan at hand, which supported them to finance their new urban living.[9] After relocation, the retail store still had limited profitability. In 2006, Yukui began to work as a small contractor in a local construction site, and his wife found a janitor's job in a cinema and entertainment center. As such, small businesses were not always more prestigious and profitable than wage work and villagers moved between the two types of jobs frequently.

Table 6.2 Private business in the sample in Ning Village

Born in	Gender	Number	1950s			1960s			1970s			1980s			1990s			2000s		
			R	C	T	R	C	T	R	C	T	R	C	T	R	C	T	R	C	T
1930s	M	2																100%		
	F	1																		
1940s	M	6												17%	17%		17%	57%		
	F	4													25%	25%	25%	50%		
1950s	M	20											5%			15%	10%	30%	10%	20%
	F	16								6%			6%			6%		38%	6%	
1960s	M	9	/	/	/	/	/	/								17%	11%	44%	22%	22%
	F	6	/	/	/	/	/	/										83%	17%	
1970s	M	8	/	/	/	/	/	/	/	/	/							25%	13%	62%
	F	6	/	/	/	/	/	/	/	/	/							17%	33%	
1980s	M	1	/	/	/	/	/	/	/	/	/	/	/	/						100%
	F	1	/	/	/	/	/	/	/	/	/	/	/	/					100%	
Not Clear	M	2	/	/	/	/	/	/	/	/	/	/	/	/						50%
	F	1	/	/	/	/	/	/	/	/	/	/	/	/				100%		
Total		83																		

R = rental business, C = commercial and retailer business, T = transportation.

Note: Among 54 couples, there were 48 men and 35 women (83 in total) who had complete working trajectory information. "/" means "not applicable" and the blank cells are used to refer to 0%.

Among different ventures, rental business remained to be an important source of income for many families. In the urbanization process, rental housing continued to be in great need. First, the locality had been a stopover for migrant workers who moved from other rural areas to search for urban jobs. Second, rural residents from the area under development mostly had to wait for shorter or longer times to be relocated after their housing was demolished, and this created a temporary demand for rental housing. Before being relocated, homeless villagers received monthly "resettlement" subsidies for temporary accommodation, and they had to look for cheap housing nearby.

Unlike cases of urban villagers encircled by the city (Liu, He, Wu, & Webster, 2010), Ning Village was completely subsumed into the city, and both their land and housing plots (*zhaijidi*) were taken away. Before that, there was little chance to capitalize housing assets that served basic needs of the family, but the urbanization process transformed them into fluid forms of capital that could be exchanged for more economic resources. However, the returns for housing investment were unstable, because self-built housing was often converted into relocation floor space at a partial rate. Some villagers managed to obtain six to eight relocation units because of their previous, spacious demolished houses, but for others, their "deserved" floor space, calculated based on the demolished housing, was quite limited, with little room that could be spared for rental business.

Constrained by their self-financing capability, some families took on debt to finance their housing purchase. This was said to serve the need of the younger generation, who would desire individual urban homes in the near future,[10] and helped to create a chance of rental business. According to respondents, it would be difficult for their children to buy new apartments whose prices kept increasing.[11] The family could use the extra housing units to generate rental incomes before their children grew up, and the monthly rent for a unit increased from 300 yuan in 2006 to 1,000 yuan in 2010. However, holding on to their multiple housing properties was not always possible and was a "difficult" path leading to future prosperity.[12] Admittedly, relocation housing usually had a lower commercial value than commodity housing, but their housing properties might bring greater returns with the real estate development of the area over time.

Along with urbanization, rental business became a reliable source of income, whereas other small commercial businesses were said to have limited profitability due to the stiffer competition in urban commercial and service sectors. Compared with other businesses, transportation businesses had increased more rapidly in the 1990s and the 2000s. This business was popular among young people, because it made them feel that they had greater freedom. Compared with other businesses, the male dominance was particularly salient in transportation. Among 14 of the interviewed families who had run a transportation business, only 2 involved both spouses, and the others were run by the husband (2 of them were run by the husband and son). Five of them bought taxis, which cost around 200,000 yuan apiece, which was hard to imagine without monetary compensations from land development. The others had chosen to buy cheaper vehicles, to pick up and transport materials for construction sites and passengers for the commercial and service centers.

Compared with the male dominance in the transportation business, the rental business created more room for women in property management. This business could be done at home and was compatible with home responsibilities. Compared with young women who had become more representative in the commercial business, middle-aged women had been well represented in running rental business. In the 2000s, the proportion of women born in the 1950s and the 1960s engaged in the rental business was higher than that of their male counterparts (38 percent to 30 percent and 83 percent to 44 percent, respectively).

Family cooperation and family division

When moving into their urban homes, the previous big families seemed to decline and family economic cooperation also became less important in the urban life in which people needed to buy commodities and services. Unlike a typical self-sufficient rural lifestyle, villagers now had to pay for food, water, electricity, and gas supplies that were of an "urban" standard and cost more. One particular living expense was for heating, which was crucial for getting through the harsh winters. Compared with the individual heating ovens that rural residences used to have, the urban apartments were equipped with a centralized heating system. Some old respondents complained that they used to collect coal for heating purposes but now needed to pay thousands of yuan per year for the "modern" heating system. This made individual earnings of cash income necessary to live an urban life. This created some difficulties for old and less educated people.

Although family cooperation became less important in coordinating economic activities, it remained important in investment and property management. Respondents mentioned that such close cooperation could be traced back to the intensification of self-built housing before land development, and both spouses worked together to have their housing decorated and rented to outsiders. To keep an eye on their rental business, some migrant workers had to put their individual jobs on hold and returned to cooperate with their spouses, and the division of labor was quite flexible in managing the rental business. After land development, some families further adjusted and diversified their property structures to seek rents. In addition to the officially sanctioned relocation housing units, some villagers used the monetary compensation to buy the first-floor shopfront rooms in the residential areas, or counters or sales rooms in the commercial centers, so that they could either use it for their own business or generate rental income.[13]

Shuping, a 36-year-old woman when interviewed in 2003, had adapted the division of labor with her husband, Tao, in property management and investment. Before land development, Tao had been a driver for a local gas station while Shuping took care of farming and household chores. In addition, they had built housing of 15 rooms and rented 14 of them, which yielded an annual income of 12,000 yuan. After land development, they bought a single-family house as their own residence and received three relocation housing units, which would be rented again. Such a rental business was the job of Shuping. Like many other villagers, they believed that women were better at communicating with tenants, and the husband was mainly involved in housing construction and maintenance of the facilities. With ample accumulations derived from the rental business, Tao bought a vehicle to run the transportation business, and he planned to start a new business by investing in a fishing pond and providing fishing services as part of the local entertainment sector.

As such, the family gained new importance in investment and property management. Unlike the dichotomous narrative in villages where some family members earned more opportunities and others were "left behind," both spouses had a chance to redirect the incomes from different family businesses into new ventures, although housing and transportation usually stood for different options preferred by the wife and the husband. In financing their investment and dealing with market uncertainties, family cooperation regained some importance with the continuing expectation of women to take care of "the inside," including the rental business.

Furthermore, the most important economic resources generated by land development, including land compensation and relocation housing, were to be claimed at the level of households. Family members had worked together to negotiate and bargain for more compensation and better deals from governments and developers. Many middle-aged women or old women were the ones in the family who went to government offices and developers' branches for the sake of family interests. For example, one old woman described that she had more time "to waste." According to her, she could "sit in front of the government office for a day, but I would not let my husband go, because it would hurt his earning chances and social status."[14] In other words, the traditional expectation of men having a more successful career was still deeply rooted, and although women were freed from the busy multitasking on farms and in sidelines, many of them continued to play a "supporting" role. Although there were more "individualized" work for young and educated people after land development, women still tried to describe themselves as being in line with expectations of being a good "homemaker." More importantly, family members were united by their common interest in a period of property boom, because properties were redistributed not based on individual rights but according to household entitlements. In other words, women had to be attached to their families (usually the marital family) to get a share of land compensation and relocation housing.

Meanwhile, in the relocation process, extended families usually split up into nuclear families. This might increase women's autonomy or "girl power," which was also an outcome of the emergence of new local employment opportunities that provided a chance for women to step out of the domestic sphere and balance family obligations and independent careers. This was added by the declining number of children that a woman expected to have. The average number of children born to a mother was 4 among women born in the 1930s and the 1940s, but it had decreased from 2.7 for the cohort born in the 1950s to 1.9 for the cohort born in the 1960s. For the younger cohorts born in the 1970s and 1980s (in their 20s and 30s around the time of our investigation), the average number was 1 (Table 6.3). Young women tended to have only one child, and

Table 6.3 Number of children in the sample in Ning Village

Mother born in	1		2		3		4		5 and more		Total	Average
1930s					33%		33%		33%		3	4
1940s					22%		56%		22%		9	4
1950s			47%		42%		5%		5%		19	2.7
1960s	25%		63%		13%						8	1.9
1970s	100%										7	1
1980s	100%										1	1
Total	10	21%	14	30%	12	26%	7	15%	4	9%	47	

Note: The number of children is missing for 7 of 54 families, and there are 47 valid cases. If the mother's age is missing, the father's age is used as an approximate. The blank cells are used to refer to 0%.

some of them mentioned the pressure generated by land development, because they would need to buy individual urban homes for each child, rather than constructing rural self-built housing at a lower cost.

The move into individual urban homes gave rise to the importance of conjugal relations but also undermined the network of mutual help between members in the extended families. Many villagers complained that the previous self-built housing was more spacious and comfortable to live in. But even when they lived separately, families remained active as a unit to fight for compensation packages for its members. Many families desired not only to have sufficient apartment units to marry off their children, but also to have some spare units to run a rental business, and the distribution of such housing resources had been relatively equal between generations and siblings.

However, family members might have diverse preferences regarding property management and investment. In some cases, women tried to persuade their husbands from investing in trendy but risky businesses and instead to save more for the family welfare and the children's education expenses. As in other societies, women might see "their interests as congruent to those of their dependent children and potentially antagonistic to those of their husbands" (Agarwal, 1997, p. 27). Both individual interests and family goals were interwoven in the process of negotiating employment and investment strategies, as well as that of dividing and reuniting the family. Some women had gained more freedom in managing their housing properties together with their husbands to generate rental income, and others had emphasized investing in their children's education for the sake of their future urban careers. Rather than seeing the livelihood strategies of rural households as well as those of women as backward and devoid of resources, Murphy (2002, p. 25) sees their employment and economic activities as resilient, adaptable, innovative, and endowed with resources.

Community in the development fever

Not only families were reorganized in living space and economic activities, the rural communities were restructured in the development fever (Song 2015).

Although peasants also welcomed improvement in the locality's lagging infrastructure and economic foundations, their "urban dream" was not as strong as in other rural areas that witnessed massive outmigration. The relatively favorable natural conditions for farming and the proximity to urban centers had made peasants less eager to escape from the rural community. Rather than the clear division between migrants and the left-behind, villagers tended to mix different kinds of economic activities to support their lives. In other words, the households' multiple job-holding practices (Van der Ploeg & Ye, 2010) helped to weave their own web of economic security. Given the passive role of the village leadership in rural industrialization and economic development, villagers relied on the family for the provision of welfare and elderly care. The rural families, however, rediscovered the importance of their attachment to and claim over land, which was a result not of pro-agriculture policies but of the anxiety of losing their land, and the desire to get more compensation in land expropriation.

Land development seemed to give rise to individual jobs rather than family-coordinated economic activities in rural areas. In a short period of time, land was expropriated and developed to attract growth-inducing investments, and villagers did not need to travel a distance to find an urban job. This seemed to accelerate an "individualization" process for those who were young and educated and could benefit from an enhanced labor market the most. Some used to be tied to land and sideline activities and felt being freed from the multitasking tasks in family cooperation and gaining a chance to develop their potential in other economic activities (like Yueqing). But for many others, the transition from family-based coordination to individual jobs was not as smooth. Many middle-aged and old peasants were not prepared for such a change, and they had limited chance of career development in the expanding urban economy.

Meanwhile, villagers often tended to evaluate whether they were losing out at the family level rather than at the individual level, as they were positioned into the property market based on household entitlements. Furthermore, such evaluation was also conducted at the community level, as the compensation and relocation package was negotiated at the team level, which had far-reaching impacts on their employment transitions. To a large extent, the changes in employment patterns had been closely related with the resistance and negotiation in land development and the formation of the insider-outsider dichotomy.

At the beginning of the development process, the village office and the team leadership had been passive followers of the development initiatives of higher authorities. Village cadres had been required by their higher authorities to help to smooth the development process. But when they were aware of the value of land and that of their own interests as a local villager, many cadres had turned from a "let-go" approach to a defending role to negotiate for better compensations. In cases of protests and petitions, the grassroots offices at the village and villagers' team levels played an intermediation role. With collective land resources, the team leadership and activists bargained for more compensation and better deals.

Local resistance and negotiation had some complicated implications for the "individualization" process brought about by urbanization. Rather than increasing the importance of the job-holding practices of individuals, it highlighted the significance of the property-holding positions by families and communities. Similar to the Minor Property Housing developments seen in many suburban villages, local people turned to village cadres as their allies, claiming their collective right to build within the rural settlement (Paik & Lee, 2012). In striving for a better livelihood, villagers saw it as a last chance to grasp a bigger share of the development revenues.

In the long run, the property-holding position was crucial for future employment opportunities, as many villagers had planned to send their children for better education using the income generated from renting or selling their properties. Although many villagers felt that they were not well prepared for the new labor market, properties they held provided some buffer time for them to survive until the smooth employment transition. In fact, many villagers had put their careers on hold to defend their property-holding positions.

Community mobilization and local resistance were not only to sooth the anxiety about property structures, but were also targeted at a better safety net, to replace the economic security that used to be provided by farming land. Although land development had created more job opportunities in the locality, many villagers did not feel economically secure to be individual earners employed by the highly profit-oriented employers. "You cannot expect much from your employers, and you may be fired at any time," said one respondent. Such a perception was also widely accepted by villagers, though they often felt that they deserved more compensation in the land development projects. Yet their dissatisfaction was mainly directed toward governments rather than "transplanted" employers, as local governments were deeply involved in approving and carrying out land development projects. Villagers had strived for larger amounts and different types of compensation, such as to raise the pension levels. Such a pension was necessary due to the fact that middle-aged villagers had concentrated in low-end jobs, and the "transplanted" employers were reluctant to provide good welfare provisions, as they did for educated urban workers. Such a safety net also helped to reduce the financial burden of the family, when villagers had no farms to grow food and needed to invest in their children in education to get a good job in the city.

Another community dynamics that affected the expectations and perceptions of the job-holding positions was the insider-outsider dichotomy. After villagers were relocated into urban residential neighborhoods, they were mixed with "outsiders," who bought the commercial housing units at the market price. This also seemed to suggest an individualization process and the dissolving of rural communities. The grassroots office of the village and the villagers' teams were replaced by residential committees, each responsible for one residential neighborhood (*xiaoqu*). The village council and party branch were retained for the transitional period to handle issues raised by villagers and to smooth the relocation process, but more grassroots offices and property management companies were settled in residential areas to serve all residents, including insiders and outsiders. Given the mixed administration system, villagers could still enjoy some of the insiders' benefits but found gradually that they were in the same or even worse standing in the expanding labor market compared with outsiders.

As with other projects of urban development and redevelopment in China driven by a desire to attract a wealthier population (He, 2007) and the governments' encouragement to demonstrate economic achievement (Yep, 2013), villagers were supposed to "make room" for development. As such, Ning Village witnessed a transition to the mixed residential pattern of locals and middle-class home purchasers from elsewhere. Being relocated to their home land, villagers felt some de facto entitlements toward the land and the local economy. However, many villagers found it was difficult to find a good job due to their age and education qualifications. Interestingly, middle-aged women were more responsive to pick up low-end local jobs after land development. Their flexibility to "fill in" in the increasingly segregated labor markets, to some extent, was related to their secondary role in the family economy, and they had less to lose in the urbanization process.

Facing an extended labor market, villagers were advantaged in starting business because they had some monetary compensation at hand, but they also complained that barriers to entry for startups had increased rapidly, given the harsh competition in the urban economy. In the tradeoff between investing in current private businesses such as transportation and in children's education for the future better urban jobs, some had chosen the latter, seeing that their businesses would have a limited profit margin. Many villagers had sent their children to universities in other cities and did not expect them to necessarily come back because "they might be able to find better jobs elsewhere." Even if they came back, they were competing with the newcomers in the same labor market, and did not enjoy an insider's advantage in seeking jobs facing the "transplanted" employers.

But most villagers still had a better propertied position than "outsiders," such as using their extra housing units to generate rental income. Although the community had limited capacity to initiate industrialization or carve out a space of employment opportunities for its indigenous residents in the urbanization process, it had managed to catch "the last train" by grabbing a share in the property boom. With regard to living expenses and investments, family resources remained important for people to strive for a better livelihood in the enhanced labor market. Although personal traits became more important in climbing up the job ladders, they could at least have a fallback position in the property market. The growing importance of property management also gave women who were in the domestic sphere more room to participate in running business, in parallel with the increase of small families after moving into urban apartments. To some extent, this empowered some women whose geographic mobility was more constrained due to their family obligations.

In sum, Ning Village had shared with other inland villages in exporting migrant labor for nonagricultural employment opportunities while keeping a foot in farming and sideline businesses before land development. Urbanization brought the labor market closer, but not necessarily more benevolent to villagers. During land development, people were not only confronted with more local employers that were transplanted to the locality, but also faced more competitors in running businesses. The imposed urbanization process left little room for conventional family businesses but gave rise to individual jobs. Meanwhile, family cooperation remained important in property management and rental business. Property structures became an important foundation of stratification between peasant families and gave rise to rental business, in which locals were considered having indigenous advantages. The two trends did empower women in different ways, by freeing educated women from less visible positions in the rural family economy to gain individual jobs, and by allowing women in the domestic sphere to invest in and run family rental businesses. However, women still shouldered more family obligations, and were more willing to take low-end jobs.

Importantly, both men and women tended to evaluate their fate not just at the individual level, but in terms of families and communities. In addition to finding independent earning opportunities, villagers still hoped to bargain for a better share in development revenues and secure a safety net given the increasing emphasis of local governments on market efficiency. The anxiety of being excluded in the modernization campaign among villagers was illustrated in the family strategies to improve their job-holding positions as well as property-holding positions.

Notes

1 Interview with the village accountant, 2003.
2 Ningxia Bureau of Statistics (Ningxia tongjiju). 2003. *Ningxia Yearbook 2003 (Ningxia tongji nianjian 2003)*. Beijing: China Statistics Press (zhongguo tongji chubanshe), p. 196.
3 Ibid.
4 Ibid.
5 Yinchuan Bureau of Statistics (Yinchuan shi tongjiju). 2010. *Yinchuan Economic and Social Development Statistics Report 2008 (Yinchuan shi 2008nian guominjingji he shehuifazhan tongjigongbao)*. Retrieved July 28, 2016 from www.tjcn.org/tjgb/201001/3334_2.html
6 Interview with Guoqing, 2002.
7 Interview with Yukui, 2005.
8 In principle, the rural land was collectively owned, and in Ning Village, the teams were the de facto holder of land, and they had adjusted family farms rather than the village office.
9 Interview with Yukui, 2005, 2006.
10 Interview with Jiao, 2009; Wangma, 2010.
11 Interview with Meng, 2006.
12 Interview with Yueqing, 2003, 2006.
13 Interview with Yukui, 2006.
14 Interview with Meng, 2006.

References

Agarwal, B. (1997). "Bargaining" and gender relations: Within and beyond the household. *Feminist Economics, 3*(1), 1–51.

Gates, H. (1996). *China's motor: A thousand years of petty capitalism*. Ithaca, NY: Cornel University Press.

He, S. (2007). State-sponsored gentrification under market transition. *Urban Affairs Review, 43*(2), 171–198.

Jacka, T. (1997). *Women's work in rural China: Change and continuity in an era of reform*. Cambridge: Cambridge University Press.

Jacka, T. (2012). Migration, householding and the well-being of left-behind women in rural Ningxia. *China Journal, 67*, 1–22.

Liu, Y., He, S., Wu, F., & Webster, C. (2010). Urban villages under China's rapid urbanization: Unregulated assets and transitional neighbourhoods. *Habitat International, 34*(2), 135–144.

Murphy, R. (2002). *How migrant labor is changing rural China*. Cambridge: Cambridge University Press.

Paik, W., & Lee, K. (2012). I want to be expropriated! The politics of Xiaochanquanfang land development in suburban China. *Journal of Contemporary China, 21*(74), 261–279.

Song, J. (2015). Space to maneuver: Collective strategies of indigenous villagers in the urbanizing region of northwestern China. *Eurasian Geography and Economics, 55*(4), 362–380.

Van der Ploeg, J. D., & Ye, J. Z. (2010). Multiple job holding in rural villages and the Chinese road to development. *The Journal of Peasant Studies, 37*(3), 513–530.

Yep, R. (2013). Containing land grabs: A mis- guided response to rural conflicts over land. *Journal of Contemporary China, 22*(80), 273–291.

7   Conclusion

Recent economic reforms have greatly reshaped the theoretical assumption of rural China as based on a small peasant economy. The evolvement of the peasant economy has resulted in the absorption of rural labor by industry (He, 2013; Wen, Dong, & Shi, 2010) on the one hand, and the trends of "capitalized agriculture" on the other hand (Yan & Chen, 2015). Existing studies have differentiated the off-farm population into migrants and local off-farm workers, and into wage laborers and entrepreneurs (Guang & Zheng, 2005; Zhao, 2004). Such trends corresponded to diverse economic strategies of villagers and their families in different areas, which interacted with gender norms in complicated ways by empowering some women but depriving others. As shown in the previous chapters, villages experienced employment changes that were shaped by the different relationship between agricultural and nonagricultural work, local and migrant work, and work outside of and inside families in the four villages.

This chapter summarizes how development models interacted with family dynamics in creating opportunities and obstacles for men's and women's employment. Although employment seems to become an individual choice, it is a combined result of negotiating rational choice, moral obligations, and gender norms and cannot be captured by the neoclassical capitalist models. In the post-socialist modernization campaign, governments and local offices play different roles, to boost the local economy by providing incentives and attracting investments, to mobilize resources by exerting the authority and regulative power, or to allow for more freedom of choice among villagers by loosening controls. The localized resource and property structures lead men and women to rely more on the family, the collective, or employers for economic security. Similar to previous findings in China (Croll, 1983; Parish & Busse, 2000), there has been a revival of the traditional division of labor. Many women retreat from the public forms of work and return to more invisible and informal work, while others find new opportunities and challenges in the market economy. Meanwhile, some women have begun to voice their individual goals and combine them with family goals in different ways.

Agricultural and nonagricultural work

In the four villages, villagers had reduced their labor investment in farming over recent decades, but with different patterns of labor moves and resource distribution given the evolvement of the farming system. A general finding in previous studies is that old generations had suffered from the poverty of the collective era and were burdened by the farming tasks given their life-course goals of constructing housing and marrying off children (Guo, 2001). Along with the opening-up of the market, the four villages witnessed different relationships between agricultural and nonagricultural work, due to the relative productivity and profitability of farming compared with other economic activities. Such changes were related with different paces of industrialization and urbanization and led to different patterns to coordinate the use of labor and resources.

Industrialization in the two coastal villages made it possible for villagers to multitask in farming and other income-generating activities at the same time without migration. Because there were plenty of local employment opportunities since the takeoff of rural industries, both men and women could be factory workers and kept farming in their "spare time," and some women reported working three shifts of factory work, farm, and family. In contrast, the families in inland villages typically combined farming and migrant work. To meet the goals of housing construction and marriage, the family usually needed to send some family members to explore economic opportunities and let the left-behind family members to keep farming. At the family level, men and young women were more active in nonfarm work that required traveling a lot, and middle-aged women tended to take more farming responsibilities as a left-behind group. The coastal and inland villages under study witnessed different patterns of holding multiple jobs, by the specialization of different family members in different tasks in inland villages, or a more mixed pattern of multitasking in coastal villages.

Under the market reform, women were the ones who tended to multitask or stay in the farming sector, but men used to play a more active role in farming when the villagers relied on collective farming as the major means to support themselves in the Maoist era. This was particularly true in Bei Village. Related with the land scarcity, women were assigned particularly low work points that discouraged them from working hard in the fields. Instead, young women were encouraged to leave agricultural tasks to men and turned to side jobs of needlework that could earn considerable income for the family. This was partly because men were perceived to be the important labor under the collective farming system and were closely monitored before the removal of institutional barriers. This ironically contributed to women's flexibility and advantage in income-earning activities, which was unique in Bei Village. Although women's labor was similarly undervalued under the collective farming system in the other villages, those women did not find alternative opportunities such as doing needlework as in Bei Village to use their "surplus" labor. In Bei Village, women's flexibility was crucial to the family's well-being and their contribution was well recognized by other family members. But such flexibility became less influential when the market opened up more opportunities for both men and women, and they began to explore more rewarding nonagricultural employment other than home-based needlework. Since then, Bei Village began to converge with other villages that quality labor tended to leave farming and became more active in the nonagricultural economic sectors

(Murphy, 2002). This reflected the job hierarchy that prioritized nonagricultural over agricultural work.

As the reform unfolded, the general decrease of labor investment in farming was manifested in two ways: to give land away or to send labor off. Villagers in the two coastal villages had been engaged in land transfer informally and formally because both genders entered nonagricultural sectors on great scales. Partly because of this, men and women had a smaller gap in moving into nonagricultural work in the two coastal villages than inland ones, although women were still more likely to multitask in farming. In Bei Village, land was first transferred to managerial farmers and then rezoned as part of the greenbelt of the city. In Su Village, both managerial farming and agricultural business contributed to the scaling-up of agriculture. Meanwhile, small farmers were marginalized in this process, and there was limited incentive for ordinary villagers to invest in farming on their remaining small plots, unless they became the managerial farmers. In the coastal villages, managerial farming could be attractive due to the favorable natural farming conditions such as rainfall and irrigation, and the enthusiasm to farm was added to by the increase of grain prices around 2004 and the government's pro-agricultural policies and subsidies since the 2000s. But such managerial farming often involved the whole family to work closely with each other on farms and made it difficult for the family to benefit from the prosperous local industries. As agricultural profits seemed less important compared with other incomes, young people in general considered farming boring, tiring, and not worthwhile.

Farming not only faded in individual interest but also was not prioritized in collective projects such as the construction of the new socialist countryside in Su Village. Under the village housing projects, the residential pattern transitioned from that of self-built housing scattered within the farm land to the concentrated and compact housing neighborhoods that were more "modern" but less farming friendly. As some respondents put it, it was not convenient to go back and forth between their new houses and farms, and many of them also needed to travel between families and factories at the same time. One village cadre admitted that agriculture was not their first concern in the community design, and they had seen industrialization as the real growth engine.[1] As more agricultural land was transferred and concentrated, some old people expressed their nostalgia for the old emotional attachment to land, but young generations often felt "freed" from farming tasks. Within the family, there were fewer typical "left-behind" members who concentrated on farming.

In inland villages, however, the decline of labor investment in farming was not so much about giving away land but more about sending some family members to migrant work and leaving other family members on the farm. Because most households had a few members involved in migrant work, they tended to be less interested and confident in running managerial farming and generating profits from it. Most families retained their land but reduced their time and energy spent on farming. Meanwhile, farming became a "lighter" job, partly achieved by the mechanization of agricultural production and the commodification of agricultural labor, and partly realized via the flexible arrangements of land use such as growing trees. Women and the elderly were still the typical family members to be left behind in agriculture, but the chance of migrant work had also increased rapidly for young women recently. The pattern used to be similar in Ning Village, but the recent land development took all the land away from villagers, which pulled all family members out of the farming sector completely.

As such, not only the structure of the farming sector but also the land development for nonagricultural uses shaped the changing relations between agricultural and nonagricultural work. It was related with different paces and patterns of urbanization in the four villages, which was in a form of rapid land development in Ning Village, in a form of gradual and partial land development in the two coastal villages, and was the least influential in Han Village. The two inland villages witnessed strong motivation to attract growth-inducing investment, but the land market had been less mature and the regulations were still in development. Depending on the governments' role in this process, Han Village and Ning Village embraced different opportunities to capitalize their land. Land transfer took place only occasionally in Han village, where some quarries rented land from villagers. The renting of land to external entrepreneurs was based on private negotiations of the use rights but the land was still collectively owned. Village cadres tended to describe it as a reasonable effort to gain a "share" from developmental revenues. By using their land in flexible ways, peasants further reduced their farming duties and made it less intensive and manageable by fewer family members. But in Ning Village, the land development involved the one-off transaction of land, and local governments played an active role in carrying out land development projects to compete with other localities in the modernization campaign. In this process, the rise of land price was perceived as reflecting achievements of economic development.

Land in the two coastal villages was partially developed for nonagricultural uses because the locality had become commercially attractive but this was constrained by government controls related to the awareness of the potential value of the rural land. The land transfer in the two coastal villages, either to facilitate managerial farming or to build the greenbelt zone, was conducted on a contract basis, and the villages remained the owners in name. As such, land compensation was calculated in a continuous way, and the affected villagers received compensation every year, which had increased over time. This was partly related to the tight land use regulations given the overall high commercial desirability of local land. In Ning Village, land compensation had also increased over time, but it was a one-off practice and villagers no longer had entitlements to land at the collective level after land development. This led to anxieties among villagers regarding how to defend their interests as "insiders."

In sum, family farms remained to provide a major fallback position for villagers due to the divide between urban cores and rural peripheries, although the divide was revised and undermined over time. Both industrialization and modernization processes reflected the valorization of a particular form of modernity (Jacka & Sargeson, 2011), in which the farming sector was to some extent assumed as backward, burdensome, and a target of improvement. Some coastal villages were industrialized and included in the modernization projects, but the zoning and construction in these villages had reinforced the agricultural-nonagricultural work hierarchy. Along with the development of nonagricultural sectors and the modern rural community, the gender gap seemed to be reduced because farming was less crucial in providing economic security and there were sufficient local jobs in nonagricultural sectors for both genders. However, women were still more likely to multitask, and there was little chance for them to conduct family farming honorably and resourcefully. Younger generations entered nonagricultural work on greater scales, and the gender gap was further reduced as they were expected to have better job prospects than their parents and were often no longer "needed" on the small plots of family farms.

In the less developed inland villages, farming continued to be a necessary but not exciting job. Due to the lack of local economic opportunities, villagers responded to the external market opportunity structures actively while there remained a minimal level of farming investment for the sake of self-sufficiency and economic security. Although the market rationality to maximize utility gained more importance in recent decades, villagers kept one foot in farming by diversifying the family labor into different economic activities to balance risks. Women continued to be more represented in the "left-behind" group, although with more opportunities as short-term agricultural laborers or part-time local workers. But young people of both genders became more mobile in general, partly because farming became "lighter."

Still, farming was not always the job for the "left-behind" women. Under certain conditions, women could be more flexible to move away from agriculture when they had home-based working opportunities to earn extra income, and men could be the ones to return to land when farming became rewarding or land became capitalized. Villagers had more autonomy to diversify their land use, and the local state allowed for more discretion at the grassroots level under the official narrative of constructing a "harmonious society." Unlike traditional morally enveloped communities (Scott, 1976) or socialist egalitarian communes, the local communities began to accommodate more diverse interests and witness great stratification among villagers, rather than tying them to the land. Given such diversification, villagers evaluated their land and adapted their attachment to land not only to the changing meaning of agriculture but also to the potential value of land accordingly.

Local and migrant work

In addition to farming, rural families in China have pursued both local and migrant work as extensions of their existing strategies for rural livelihood diversification (Murphy, 2002). Unlike their urban counterparts who typically obtain jobs based on individual qualifications, rural migrant workers were often engaged in temporary and unstable jobs in which they were seen as cheap, docile, or nimble manual laborers. But for villages that exported labor, it was usually the quality labor that tended to be more mobile and leave the villages. In coastal areas where villagers could find nonfarm work in their local communities, the hierarchical dichotomy of migrant workers and the left-behind was undermined by the prevalence of local work. The different combinations of local and migrant work in different villages were closely related with the different experiences and expectations for men and women and of different generations.

The divide between the migrants and the left-behind was more significant in inland villages where local nonfarm jobs were limited. The eagerness to earn immediate income was particularly salient in the early reform years, which led to massive labor outmigration among men and young women. However, it did not lead to a complete shift of "de-peasantization" but the half-proletarian status of peasants (Pun & Lu, 2010), which implied their continuing connections with the rural base and unstable relations with urban labor regimes. There was also limited local work as well, such as that of "going up to the mountain" in Han Village, which was often more casual but less rewarding than migrant work. Such local jobs were limited given the underdevelopment of local entrepreneurial dynamics, which was undermined due to the threat of external capital. The market squeeze also led to the search for the cheapest and most docile laborers from the more "inland" areas by the capitalist forces in Han Village.

In Han Village, either "going to Beijing" or "going up to the mountain" was conventionally men's work. Men had advantages in both local and migrant work because women were discouraged from traveling afar or transporting stones, but the male dominance in migrant work was more salient. The most important danger for women was perceived to be the corrupting market forces when they were away from home. As such, women had been more likely to take part in local rather than migrant work in the early reform years, although the local job opportunities for women were also very limited, such as helping in local workshops or cooking for quarries, which was added to by the emergence of home-based sideline work in the 1990s. But over time, women became more active in migrant work, although still mostly in their 20s. Only a few women could continue their migrant work, when there were grandmothers, usually the paternal grandmothers, who could help with the family and farming obligations for young women. Their extended migration experiences were also facilitated by migrating together with their husbands to the cities, as a factor that counteracted risks in the city and in the labor market.

The gender difference was also manifested in different choices over the life stages and between generations. Men were active in both local and migrant work, and they were mostly active in migrant work in their 20s and then sometimes in their 40s, related to their life cycle timing to construct their own and their sons' housing. But over cohorts, young men tended to concentrate more in migrant work. This intergenerational change was more salient among women, who had a lower starting point to begin with. This was not only related to the rise of more diverse job opportunities in the external labor market compared with the limited jobs provided by local quarries, but also due to a greater exposure to urban consumerism and the modern social media. Although the expectations on men as the major breadwinner remained relatively stable, the expectations on women, particularly for daughters-in-law, had changed over time. Some young women benefited particularly from the family strategies of tied migration, but for old women, there remained limited job opportunities both in local and in migrant work. Old women were the ones who helped in domestic work and farming for young women, although not all of the young women could get such help, related with the common residential patterns that parents lived with the youngest son and his small family. As such, women witnessed a sharp but contingent increase in migrant work over generations.

The local–migrant divide has been restructured fundamentally in the two coastal villages, where migrant work declined rapidly when most villagers were absorbed into local industries. In both villages, the expansion of rural industries even led to the influx of migrant workers from inland areas. In Su Village, such immigrants mainly concentrated at the bottom of the labor market in the several big enterprises, and the expansion of the enterprises also allowed for greater upward mobility for the young and educated local people. In Bei Village, the small rural industries did not generate many of such opportunities, and some most "capable" laborers had tended to leave the wage sector to run private businesses. In both villages, the local–migrant divide of work and the related urban-rural gap were greatly challenged due to the prosperity of rural industries, but their different development patterns led to the distinct job hierarchies, in which local wage work was more favorable in Su Village and private businesses in Bei Village.

Even in villages where local jobs were easily available, men and women were still often recruited for different positions with the perceived female's advantage in nimble and repetitive work and the male's advantage in technical work. As the market reform unfolded, the new gender division emerged in Su Village that men were more likely to take salesperson or managerial positions that required traveling and networking, and women were more represented in locally based clerical and accounting positions. In Bei Village, women became more represented in local wage work because men, especially the resourceful men, were more likely to turn to the private sectors. Although some women also experienced such transitions, men were perceived to be more suitable for such risk-taking activities. Although the dual-earner pattern was more prevalent compared with the two inland villages under study, there were more complicated gendered divides underlying the seemingly egalitarian working patterns in the two coastal villages.

Unlike coastal villages where industrialization played a big role in creating local work, urbanization made a big difference in the two inland villages in generating job opportunities. Through the development of new office buildings, commercial centers, and industrial sectors in the recent urbanization process in Ning Village, villagers faced an enhanced local labor market, while land development also deprived people of the traditional means to guarantee economic security. Driven by anxiety, many men put on hold their migrant jobs to return home to "watch the land" and to construct more housing, so that the family could be better compensated following land expropriation and housing demolition. This led to some "reverse" cases that men became less mobile than women, because housing construction and land watching became the most important jobs for the local families. Meanwhile, some women began to take up some migrant jobs in the urban service sectors to make up the cash income for the families. Such a gender divide was transitional, and was replaced by the dominance of local work for both men and women after urbanization was completed. But such a transitional gender divide still suggested that men tended to do the most important jobs for the families, and women often took up work that made "supplementary" incomes and resources.

In sum, migrant work remained important for inland villagers, and its relationship with local work often overlapped with that of the coastal–inland dichotomy and the urban-rural divide. Coastal villagers relied more on local work, which was more available and desirable, as rural industries had been better recognized in the job hierarchies over time. The gender gap had been more salient in inland villages due to the lack of local employment opportunities and the expectation for women to be less mobile. However, the gender difference could be revised and reversed unexpectedly under the rapid urbanization and evolve over time to allow more mobility for young women. In sum, young men and women not only moved out of agriculture more completely but also moved on to market opportunities adaptively with new aspirations. But still, the male advantage continued in terms of taking jobs that required traveling a lot and taking risks.

Career ladders and family cooperation

Market reforms have led to different trends of villagers to become employees in the market or be family-based producers, which were combined in different forms in the villages under study. In line with a tradition of populist understanding of the peasant economy, the family farming system and the small holding of land had provided some room for petty commodity producers. But the development of petty commodity production was contingent on the diverse industrialization and urbanization processes, and villagers had adapted their family division of labor to the rising rural industries or the subsumption of urban capital. This helped to shape different mechanisms of economic mobility and career development, as reflected in work inside and outside the family with its gendered patterns.

Many villagers had been absorbed in the extra-household economic activities either in local industries or migrant work, but with different expectations and experiences of career development. In inland villages, their industries were either underdeveloped, marginalized, or taken over by external capital. Villagers still had some hope of self-development in their migrant work, by relating it with the urban lifestyle, modern production, and the consumerist culture. But at the same time, migrant workers found that it was difficult to climb up the career ladders in the urban workplaces, partly constrained by their education and partly related to their migrant status. Some migrant workers regretted that they had not prolonged their educations, but that had been difficult given the concentration of education resources in cities. Despite the poor rural education environment, their families usually could not afford to send them to good urban schools, which could have laid a good foundation for their future career development.[2]

Related with that, many migrant workers had limited career aspirations and saw their work as leading to nowhere. To some extent, the harsh working conditions and the market uncertainties reinforced the gendered employment pattern where men's migration work was vital to satisfy the family needs, and women's mobility was less encouraged and more contingent on family factors. Even for young generations in which the gender gap decreased in their representation in migrant work, it was still difficult to develop migrant work into a lifelong career. The limited career prospects in wage work sometimes encouraged inland villagers to turn to their own businesses if allowed by their resources.

Due to the limited resources, private businesses in Han Village were often built on the collaboration of several families, or characterized by the male-bonding culture. This led to the differentiation of "men's business" (quarries and transportation), which often required taking risks, traveling over distances, and building brotherhood relationships, and "women's business" (stores and barbershops) that involved mainly individual work. It was perceived to be appropriate and feasible for men to mobilize resources via networking, which to some extent constrained women's role in managing properties and businesses.

Villagers in Ning Village faced similar difficulties in the labor market but were more ready to conduct private businesses because of their newly propertied positions in urbanization. Among the companies and other employers that were established after urbanization, many were transplanted from elsewhere and were not originally locally based as in Su Village and were not obligated to help local villagers in their transition to local work and urban life. Although villagers were no longer disadvantaged by their migrant status in workplaces, they faced stiffer competition in an enhanced labor market. Although these enterprises and companies had institutionalized career ladders, villagers found that the upward mobility opportunities were reserved for young and educated people. Most villagers were welcomed in the rising low-end urban jobs in service and construction sectors, such as construction workers, gardeners, security guards, and janitors. To a large extent, urbanization had reinforced the stratification in the labor market based on age and education, and it also continued the gender politics that old women illustrated more flexibility to earn supplementary incomes without high expectations to move up the career ladders.

Meanwhile, villagers were better prepared in starting businesses based on monetary compensation and housing they received. Among the different kinds of ventures, the gender gap was smaller in commercial and rental businesses but greater in transportation businesses. This was because the former ventures often involved a close collaboration of spouses, and women were often perceived to be suitable in communicating with clients and tenants in these kinds of businesses, which did not require traveling a lot. As such, the family businesses created some room for women to play a role in managing properties and operating ventures. Rental incomes helped many families to finance their new urban lives, and they put hope on the young generation of both genders to get a decent job in the enhanced labor market.

Villagers were positioned in different kinds of career ladders in the local industries in the two coastal villages. The first generation of factory workers in the nascent rural industries relied more on their local networks and organizational links to get a job in the village's factories. Meanwhile, there were some collective working teams or craftsmen's teams that sought collective patronage and were incorporated into the collective economy. In building their own factories, some villagers became managers and technicians, which formed the foundation of a new group of economic elites in the countryside. In contrast, rural migrant workers mainly worked as cheap manual laborers in urban factories and rarely had such chances for career development.

In Su Village, the career ladders for local cadres and factory managers had largely overlapped under the coordination of the village office. The village leadership mobilized capable youth to participate in public affairs and contribute to the collective economy, and they were the candidates for either village cadres or factory managers. Many rural factory managers had advantages on both sides in that they were able to cultivate organizational links within the village on the one hand and connections with the urban technicians and clients on the other hand. Such networking and technical skills, which were perceived as crucial characteristics of political and economic elites, were related with a male dominance in the upward mobility in the nascent rural industries. Only a few women who were the "iron girls," exemplary laborers, or political stars could achieve recognition and play a leading role in rural industrialization.

The overlapping of the dual career ladders of cadres and managers declined in an increasingly privatized economy. The privatization process created a new class of economic elites, including previous mangers who became private entrepreneurs, and managerial and white-collar workers who climbed the career ladder largely based on their human capital. The connections with the village leadership were no longer so important in getting promoted in the big enterprises, and the cadres had less influence on the operation of the privatized enterprises. In response, the local state adopted a new co-optation strategy to make the most successful entrepreneurs into political "stars," and induce them to join the village leadership and to maintain a close connection with the local community. Male dominance in the entrepreneurial and political leadership continued, as many collective managers, mostly male, took the entrepreneur position after privatization.

The new stratification system in the privatized rural industries led to the changing expectations among people from relying on the collective to get a factory job to seeking a decent job in the big enterprises based on their age and education. Such stratification took place not only according to the dichotomy of local villagers and migrant workers from inland villages, but with new gender and generational differences in opportunities of career development. Within the group of local laborers, young and educated people faced more opportunities to move upward to white-collar and managerial positions than the old generations who spent their young ages muddling through the market rather than prolonging their education. For old local people, the chance to move upward was limited, but they were not fired easily even at the floor-level positions. This formal institution of career ladders embedded in the rural community created some opportunities for young and educated women similar to that of their male counterparts. Compared with family businesses in which women's contribution was sometimes devalued and invisible, a formal job made a good excuse for young women to be exempted from the traditional expectations of household responsibilities. Meanwhile, old women tended to help with the domestic work to facilitate the career development of young women. Because most villagers had relied on employers rather than families for economic security, family cooperation mainly occurred in the field of care work rather than economic activities.

Family cooperation and accumulations were more important in Bei Village, because of the limited room to have career development in the wage sectors and the persisting aspiration of running one's own business. Bei Village also witnessed an early rural industrialization, but with a more prevalent tradition of family sidelines and craftsmanship, and people needed to make deposit investment to enter collective enterprises. Rural industries had been relatively small compared with Su Village, which was related with the limited chances of upward mobility. Many villagers left the wage sectors in the 1990s, and this period was perceived to be the best time to start one's business. The rising aspiration of running one's own business made the private sector more prestigious than factory jobs, and people ranked being a boss over working for others.[3] In Su Village, however, it was still the norm to enter a factory rather than relying on private accumulations of economic resources to achieve economic success.

In Bei Village, where family economic cooperation became more prevalent, women might become inside coordinators, whereas in Su Village, given the ample local formal work opportunities and the chances of promotion, women usually pursued an independent career separate from that of other family members, and their connections with employers were more important for economic security. In Su Village, the career prospects for old women were more limited than those for young women, and thus they took on flexible work schedules and contributed to the egalitarian division of labor among young couples. In Bei Village, such a generational gap in career development was less significant due to the small sizes of rural industries, and the intergenerational cooperation in housework was more ambiguous.

Throughout the Maoist era, the possible channels of moving upward and moving across the urban-rural boundaries, such as going to universities and joining the military service, were limited. Under the market reform, the chances of upward mobility emerged via different mechanisms based on collective patronage, human capital, and private accumulations. In inland villages, the rural-to-urban labor migration did create some chances of spatial mobility, but still with limited chances of upward mobility. Even after Ning Village was rapidly urbanized, villagers continued to have limited career prospects in an expanded local labor market but more opportunities to develop their businesses given the capitalization of their land and housing. Women were still less mobile in the labor market, but they had exerted their agency to enhance their participation with certain compromises, such as migrating with their husbands, taking up the less desirable jobs in the urbanized areas, and helping with renting and managing properties.

The career ladders were most institutionalized and serving the locals' interests in career development in Su Village. Along with the privatization process, employers began to converge with the capitalist profit orientation of private enterprises, but most villagers could still access individual wage work in local industries with an enhanced chance of upward mobility. In Bei Village, the importance of wage work in local industries was undermined by the prosperity of private businesses based on individual accumulations or family cooperation. Despite the male dominance in such risk-taking ventures, women sometimes used their flexible strategies to achieve economic success, such as by drawing on resources of their natal families or becoming internal managers in their husbands' businesses.

Family dynamics and development models

The different industrialization and urbanization processes had resulted in distinct local economic structures, in which different family strategies of multiple job holding were developed to balance rewards and risks. The two inland villages were dominated by the construction and transportation economy, which was related with the specialization of men in these economic activities and women's concentration in other economic segments. The two coastal villages prospered based on the development of "light" industries such as textile and other manufacturing sectors, in which both men and women were active, and some family members split their working time to multitask in farming and other economic tasks, which was more common among women. In Ning Village and Bei Village, where families had access to more resources either due to urbanization or industrialization, the cooperation of different family members in the same private business was also commonly observed.

At the family level, trying and holding multiple jobs seemed to echo the conventional rural household economy based on mixed sources of income, but this was a combined result of the declining institutional barriers of labor migration and rural industrialization, as well as the recent campaign of modernization. For example, the growth spurt of rural industries in the coastal villages was driven by locally owned capital, in opposition to urban-industrial capital. But compared with the formal urban jobs, rural wage jobs were perceived to be informal and less prestigious at the beginning, and the related market uncertainties made multiple job holding a reasonable choice. Similarly, inland rural families usually let their most capable family members do migrant work, but they also continued to combine different sources of income. After urbanization, many families continued to hold on to multiple jobs due to the limited safety nets and the stiffer market competition, such as combining wage work and rental business.

At the same time, different development models created diverse patterns of individualized work, and for the young generation, multiple job holding became less important as they were more attracted to the "modern" economic sectors.

Women used to be the ones in the family who took the flexible or "left-behind" roles in the family's multiple job holding strategies, but such gender divide was sometimes reduced by the intergenerational division of labor that old people took care of the less important and less visible economic and family tasks. Such adaptive strategies challenged the populist theorization of the conflict between outside capital and internal peasant developments that failed to account for the differentiation among peasants through the lens of a unified peasantry (Yan & Chen, 2015).

In the diffusion of resources and job opportunities, stratification took place based on personal traits, as well as the persisting inequalities and developmental politics. In this process, the roles of the local state and the family economy were important in shaping development models and employment choices. The interaction of developmental politics and gender relations combined to shape how resources and job opportunities were generated and distributed to serve development goals and the gender ideology.

In Ning Village, urbanization was part of the municipal development strategy. The city and district governments played an important role in designing the development plan and attracting investors and employers. Given the primary target of boosting the local economy, the newly developed industrial and commercial zones created more individualized work and demanded quality labor, and local villagers had to compete in an enhanced labor market with newcomers with few "indigenous" advantages. Because the goal of gender equality was not prioritized in the modernization campaign, the gender division of labor was largely a result of family coordination and market competition. Women were sometimes empowered with the access to individualized work outside home, but their adaptive move to take up the low-end jobs, mostly among middle-aged women, reinforced their devalued position in the labor market. Meanwhile, women's participation in the commercial and rental business added to their agency in accessing resources and managing properties, but with little chance in the male-dominated transportation business.

In contrast, Han Village witnessed little influence of the local state in designing and promoting the modernization campaign. Given the dismantling of the collective economy and the fiscal reform in the 1990s that reduced the tax revenue bases for local administration, the village office had limited resources and had difficulties implementing the macro-level policies to improve basic welfare systems and to promote the urban-rural integration. What the village office could do was to provide more room for villagers to take advantage of the institutional and policy ambiguities for their own interests, and also to absorb discontents and avoid conflicts with villagers under a new official narrative of constructing "harmonious" society. Village cadres kept one eye closed to those who grew trees and received pro-agriculture subsidies, those who rented their land to quarries, and those who reached private agreements of compensation for the noises and pollution generated by the quarry industry. Such local discretion was to allow villagers to deal with economic insecurity and to take advantage of different economic opportunities.

Even the village office itself relied on renting quarries as one of the few ways to add to their budget. Some peasants complained that the village leadership was weak or corrupt in the face of external capital and was incapable of defending the indigenous economic interests from relentless market forces. But others were satisfied with receiving rents or compensation directly from private entrepreneurs, and they did not want the village collective to step in to take a share. Meanwhile, the limited authority and regulative power of the village office were related with the presence of the nearby big cities, including Beijing. Han Village had been a pool of cheap laborers and a supplier of construction materials for these big cities, but their migrant workers were also perceived to be a backward productive force that sometimes needed to be sent back for the sake of the "city image." As such, the local state had a limited role to play in addition to serving the development plan of big cities. The absence of an interventionist local state and the persisting patrilocal family structures made labor migration continue to be a gendered process, due to the perceived differences for men and women regarding their capabilities to deal with market uncertainties and other risks.

But young women's earning capacity was also well recognized in recent decades, which was facilitated by the presence of grandparents at home and the tied migration with their partners. Just as sons with different sibling orders might leave the extended family at different times, individual women's labor participation was part of the family strategies conditioned by life cycles. In a "householding" process, family members conducted different activities inside and outside home to balance migrant labor and agriculture, to sustain the family, and to keep workloads bearable (Jacka, 2012). Compared with older generations, young men and women unprecedentedly indulged in urban consumerism and commercial culture, while they still could not easily escape rurality via the seemingly individualization process. To deal with the lack of resources and opportunities, people had relied on either the male-bonding networks to mobilize resources or the "householding" processes to allow young men and women to leave the village for better economic opportunities. Different from the "girl power" narrative of a confrontational relationship that young women were empowered to challenge their mothers-in-law, old women helped to free young women from housework and childrearing responsibilities. Due to the lack of government and collective coordination in developing a growth engine, family coordination and personal networks played an important role in shaping the employment patterns between genders and across generations.

The development engine at the village level played a more important role in Su Village. Rather than seeing the morally enveloped rural communities as protecting the peasant economy from market expansions and state extractions, the village leadership had actively initiated industrialization. To some extent, villagers were in a local favorable market environment instead of a wider external market. Employers continued to favor local people rather than migrant workers but also recruited and promoted people based on merit and connections. On the one hand, local wage jobs were more favorably regarded, given the greater opportunities for career development. On the other hand, such jobs were still related with economic security and in line with the ideal womanhood. As a combined result, both local men and women benefited considerably from employment opportunities in such a corporatist development model.

However, this does not mean the corporatist development model coordinated by the village leadership always helped to promote equal employment opportunities for men and women. The case of Daqiu suggested that women could also be squeezed from the paid labor force given the collective-dominated heavy industries. Even in Su Village, which was dominated by light industries, the seeming gender equality in wage work was based on the generational differences of labor use and the influx of migrant workers from outside, which suggested the other inequalities underlying the "girl power" enjoyed by local young women.

When local young men and women gained more opportunities to move up the career ladders, more migrant workers filled in the floor-level jobs in factories. Some respondents proudly commented on the better economic opportunities for both genders among local villagers and used gender equality as a sign of their more "developed" status.[4] Despite the continuing dominance of men in entrepreneurial, managerial, and salesperson positions, such gender differences were largely ignored or masked by the sense of superiority of locals over migrant workers.

Similarly taken for granted were the different opportunities of self-development for young and old women in the corporatist development model. Old women had spent their young ages with the virtue of "enduring bitterness" to contribute to both the public and the private spheres. Although women were encouraged to overcome their biological obstacles to become honorable laborers and exemplars, only a few women managed to become stars in public and labor participation. Over time, women's contributions were evaluated more by bringing home wages given the development of the local light industries and the evolvement of agriculture. Nowadays, even old people were less bound to farming tasks, as the village coordinated land transfer for the purpose of managerial farming or nonagricultural use. Some old people still had a wage job in factories that were reserved for the aged group and paid less, compared with their educated young adult children. From a family point of view, it became rational for many old women to give up their wage jobs to help with the household responsibilities of young women, especially when the daughter or daughter-in-law had a decent position and promising income in her workplace, but this generational division occurred less frequently for men, related to the traditional beliefs about women's responsibility in domestic work.

As such, developmental politics interacted with gender relations with the intermediation of family dynamics. In other words, the corporatist development model did not necessarily undermine the significance of family in coordinating labor use but changed the forms of the family division of labor in important ways. In the villages under study, the decline of the socialist collective economy was accompanied by a renewed focus on household-based production, sometimes through the division between migrant work in urban cores and care work in the countryside and sometimes via the mobilization of family resources to develop private businesses. To a large extent, families remained to be an ultimate welfare provider for villagers.

The importance of the household utility had to be embedded in the reshuffling job hierarchies that regarded working for others and working for oneself more or less desirable. Subject to capital intensiveness, private business could rank higher or lower than wage work. In Su Village, the diversification of wage work positions made it possible for villagers to pursue career development via individualized work rather than based on family resources, and the young and educated women could be empowered considerably by their independent earning power. In Bei Village, private businesses were generally more prestigious, and families had become important actors to mobilize resources and conduct market adventures. The diverse development models suggested a different relationship between the household utility and individual achievements, which could not be captured by the unitary household model and the materialistic approach that emphasized individual market success as the basis of women's empowerment.

China's rural policies continued to use families as a basic unit of peasant production. Just as the official narrative "allowing someone to get rich first and reaching common prosperity eventually," the resources and opportunities families got were assumed to benefit all family members eventually. But women's entitlement was often compromised by the existing kinship and marriage system (Fforde, 1999). For example, policies of land use often focused on families and seemed gender neutral, but failed to account for the relationship of individual entitlements under the unitary household model (Bélanger & Xu, 2009). This called for a bargaining model that could provide more insights into the interaction of self-interests within the family (Bélanger & Xu, 2009).

While the cash-income measure became the major base for young women to fight for "fairness" and equality relationships in Su Village, they did not use "labor" but "money" as grounds for claiming more bargaining power, as found in other studies (Huang, 2011). This seemed to support the crude materialist model, but the involvement of old women in paid work did not lead to their claim for equal sharing of household responsibilities, which was an unpaid "women's job" that counted less. Admittedly, old women could also use it to remind their family of what they had done for them and thus enhance their security in the family (Huang, 2011). Many young women had felt gratitude and sympathy toward their mothers or mothers-in-law for their self-sacrifice and hard work. This could be a source of security different from the bargaining power that was built on the equivalent earning power, but such a source of power should not be exaggerated. Despite the narrowed gender gap and the increased value of daughters, patriarchy was revised and reserved via the flexible intergenerational division of labor.

Family roles were more important in economic terms in a context of the rising private sectors in Bei Village. Such private sectors could have evolved from the courtyard economy or the specialized household businesses in which women might take a lead, but such businesses were sometimes taken over by their husbands when they were developed to a certain level (Jacka, 1997). But in Bei Village, women's roles were more diverse and remained important in the various forms of private businesses. Some women helped in their husbands' family businesses with a less visible role, but some other women conducted their own businesses with the resources provided by their natal family. Even in the businesses based on the husband-wife partnership, some women learned to exert their agency and carve out their room for autonomy.

The different family cooperation patterns suggested the necessity to examine the complicated relationship between individual and family goals in negotiating employment that was masked by the unitary household model. Unlike the intergenerational division of labor where old women helped young women in family responsibilities, some middle-aged and old women chose to pursue their individualistic employment opportunities. For example, Suqin's mother-in-law refused to take care of the grandson because she was occupied by her own wage job and prioritized her own incomes over the family goal (for the extended family). Sometimes it was the young women who wanted to be in charge of how to raise their children, as Haiping suggested, and for that purpose she would rather put her own career on hold. The increasing focus on individual achievements and happiness added more complexities in how the family negotiated employment patterns. Young women might or might not rely on old women to take care of family responsibilities, and the gender divide was not always reduced by intergenerational differences.

Although the market economy created opportunities for both men and women to participate in new market-oriented activities (Bossen, 2002, p. 144), attitudes toward women's work remained ambiguous and left room for continuous negotiation of employment for both genders in the family. Women's image had become more diverse since the decline of the officially praised image of "strong" women in the Maoist era. Even at that time, only a narrowly selected group of "capable" women could play a leading role in local economic activities. Nowadays women were no longer encouraged to compete directly with men and gain public recognition via self-sacrifice and hard work. Young women had been mostly exempted from the hardship of farm work, and they did not share the honorable memory of women making a difference in the public sphere, nor were they interested in being "strong" women. More often, they moved into the "modern" economic sectors based on their education, skills, and connections, rather than the virtues of enduring bitterness and overcoming biological obstacles. As it became ideologically acceptable for women to return home or work intermittently, the gender differences in taking challenging and risk-taking jobs were more pronounced. Some young women highlighted their emotional desire to be a good mother, which served their self-satisfaction (Song, 2015). In particular, the devotion of socialist heroines and exemplars who sacrificed family life for public interests was considered "foolish," and the emphasis on the interests of their families and children was more in line with women's personal satisfaction and happiness.

Such trends reinforced gender inequalities in many aspects. The retreat of women from the public sphere was parallel with the fact that the elite entrepreneurs and political stars were predominantly male. As suggested by some respondents who were female cadres, they felt their impacts were trivial, their positions were not taken seriously, and political capital bore more symbolic than materialistic meanings for women. With the perception of women as nimble, docile, and with less technical sophistication, women's labor was perceived as important in generating incomes but was still devalued in different ways. But at the same time, women have taken advantage of the new economic opportunities by adopting flexible employment patterns without necessarily breaking existing gender norms and expectations. Both old and young women might not challenge the gender division of labor at home directly, but tried to "find the many sites of power and resistance" to "achieve success in their lives" (Riley, 2012, p. 137). Their power could be "rooted in the family" (Riley, 2012, p. 137), such as to become the "family manager" of the business. Some other women emphasized self-fulfillment to a greater extent, which could be built on independent career pursuits or good motherhood, and be balanced by working intermittently. To them, the temporary retreat or putting their career on hold was not just merely a disruption to their careers but could also suggest some deliberate decisions with certain compromises and the employment outcomes needed to be evaluated in the long run. To some extent, these trends did not fit the materialist model that directly related women's emancipation with their independent labor participation outside home. This marked a shift from women's honored virtues of hard work and bitter endurance to an emphasis on individual happiness and self-development, sometimes in line with the goals and interests of other family members and sometimes not. Such flexible and strategic forms of gendered employment patterns have to be contextualized in different development models.

Notes

1 Interview with Xiaoping, 2010.
2 Some mentioned that rural schools had "poor education quality," and teachers were not even working hard to retain students. Thus it was difficult for rural children to go to universities or get good degrees. See interview with Haitao, 2008.
3 When asked about the job ranks in the two villages, people in Bei Village put "bosses" (people who had their own businesses, either small or big) in the first place, then managers, cadres and professionals, then people with other salaried jobs, and finally peasants with no other jobs; people in Su Village, however, ranked the managers in big enterprises first, then professionals and local officials, then people having their own ventures, and finally peasants with no other jobs. In other words, formal and stable work was most valued in Su Village, while people in Bei Village envied those who "take big risks and earn big money." See interview with Yu, 2005; Jianxin, 2010.
4 Interview with Weidong, 2010; Fengdan, 2010.

References

Bélanger, D., & Xu, L. (2009). Agricultural land, gender and kinship in rural China and Vietnam: A comparison of two villages. *Journal of Agrarian Change, 9*(2), 204–230.
Bossen, L. (2002). *Chinese women and rural development.* Lanham, MD: Rowman and Littlefield.

Croll, E. J. (1983). *Chinese women since Mao*. New York: Zed.

Fforde, A. (1999). The transition from plan to market: China and Vietnam compared. In J. Benedict, K. Tria, C. Anita, & U. Jonathan (Eds.), *Transforming Asian socialism: China and Vietnam compared* (pp. 43–72). Canberra: Allen and Unwin.

Guang, L., & Zheng, L. (2005). Migration as the second-best option: Local power and off-farm employment. *The China Quarterly, 181*, 22–45.

Guo, Y. H. (2001). Daiji guanxi zhong de gongping luoji jiqi bianqian – Dui Hebei nongcun yanglao moshi de fenxi (The logic of fairness and transition in intergenerational relations – an analysis of elderly care patterns in rural Hebei Province). *Zhongguo xueshu, 4*, 221–254.

He, X. F. (2013). *Xiaonong lichang (Small peasant stance)*. Beijing: China University of Political Science and Law Press.

Huang, Y. (2011). Labour, leisure, gender and generation: The organization of "wan" and the notion of "gender equality" in contemporary rural China. In T. Jacka & S. Sargeson (Eds.), *Women, gender and rural development in China* (pp. 49–70). Cheltenham, UK: Edward Elgar Publishing.

Jacka, T. (1997). *Women's work in rural China: Change and continuity in an era of reform*. Cambridge: Cambridge University Press.

Jacka, T. (2012). Migration, householding and the well-being of left-behind women in rural Ningxia. *China Journal, 67*, 1–22.

Jacka, T., & Sargeson, S. (Eds.). (2011). *Women, gender and rural development in China*. Northampton, MA: Edward Elgar Publishing.

Murphy, R. (2002). *How migrant labor is changing rural China*. Cambridge: Cambridge University Press.

Parish, W. L., & Busse, S. (2000). Gender and work. In W. F. Tang & W. Parish (Eds.), *Chinese urban life under reform* (pp. 209–231). Cambridge: Cambridge University Press.

Pun, N., & Lu, H. L. (2010). Unfinished proletarianization: Self, anger and class action of the second generation of peasant-workers in reform China. *Modern China, 36*(5), 493–519.

Riley, N. E. (2012). *Gender, work, and family in a Chinese economic zone: Laboring in paradise*. Wiesbaden: Springer Science & Business Media.

Scott, J. C. (1976). *The moral economy of the peasant*. New Haven, CT: Yale University Press.

Song, J. (2015). Women and self-employment in post-socialist rural China: Side job, individual career or family venture. *The China Quarterly, 221*, 229–242.

Wen, T. J., Dong, X., & Shi, Y. (2010). Zhongguo nongye fazhan fangxiang de zhuanbian he zhengce daoxiang: Jiyu guoji bijiao yanjiu de shijiao (The change in the direction of Chinese agricultural development and policy guidance). *Problems of Agriculture Economy (Nongye jingji wenti), 10*, 88–93.

Yan, H. R., & Chen, Y. Y. (2015). Agrarian capitalization without capitalism? Capitalist dynamics from above and below in China. *Journal of Agrarian Change, 15*(3), 366–391.

Zhao, L. T. (2004). *Path to private entrepreneurship: Markets and occupational mobility in rural China*. Unpublished doctoral dissertation, Stanford University, U.S.

Index